TAKE IT FROM THE TOP

TAKE IT FROM THE TOP

An Autobiographical Scrapbook

HUMPHREY LYTTELTON

Drawings by the author

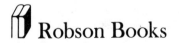 Robson Books

FIRST PUBLISHED IN GREAT BRITAIN IN 1975 BY
ROBSON BOOKS LTD., 28 POLAND STREET,
LONDON W1V 3DB. COPYRIGHT © 1975 HUMPHREY
LYTTELTON.

ISBN 0 903895 56 0

Some of the chapters in this book draw on material which
originally appeared in *Punch* and *Harpers and Queen*. We are
grateful to the editors of these magazines for permission to
include it.

Photoset, printed and bound in Great Britain by
Redwood Burn Limited, Trowbridge & Esher

CONTENTS

I WAS ONCE attendant upon Duke Ellington at his suite in the Dorchester Hotel when he was having breakfast. It was four o'clock in the afternoon when, in the other world of offices, factories, cricket grounds and suburban households, everything stops for tea. But the Duke was having breakfast. It consisted of fruit juice, steak with salad, cheese, fruit salad and coffee, and he ate it—if I may borrow a dimly-remembered technical term from schoolroom physics—not in series but in parallel. In other words, he cleared the way with a gulp of fruit juice, took in a slice of steak, followed it in rapid succession with a liberal spoonful of fruit salad and a wedge of cheese, washed the lot down with coffee, then went on to another permutation.

He only finished half the huge steak. The other half he wrapped carefully in a paper napkin and put in the fridge. Billy Strayhorn, his friend, collaborator and chancellor, saw my eyebrows go up. 'Duke knows about touring in England,' he said. 'He likes to put something by for the middle of the night.' 'What happens in hotels where they have no fridge?' I asked. 'He puts it out on the window ledge.'

Here, I thought, must be the patron saint of all touring jazzmen, a man who combined a keen and idiosyncratic appreciation of the good things of life with a healthy regard for self-preservation. He loved music, words, food and laughter. Since this book involves all of these, I humbly dedicate it to St. Edward Kennedy Ellington.

H.L.

R.I.P.

HUMPHREY LYTTELTON, the well-known Old Etonian ex-Guards Officer jazz trumpeter, was born on May 23rd, 1921 at Eton, the only son (among four daughters) of an Eton school-master. It was, many observers agree, the turning-point in his career. Up till then he had led what can only be described as a sheltered life, taking little active part in public life and relying heavily in most matters affecting his livelihood upon his mother. It is not known exactly when he came to a decision about a career, but it is safe to say that, at an age when the average, healthy boy is grappling with the choice between growing up to be an engine-driver or a sex maniac, Lyttleton had already decided that for him it was to be a well-known Old Etonian ex-Guards Officer jazz trumpeter.

To be born on May 23rd, 1921 at Eton, the only son of an Eton schoolmaster, was a brilliant first step in a career marked by many examples of such forethought and inspiration. The location and circumstances speak for themselves. It was one of the dispensations of Henry VI Our Founder, his heirs and successors, that the son of an Eton master should be educated at the College free, gratis and for no more than it takes to equip him with a top hat, a suit of tails, two sets of underwear and an allowance of seven and sixpence a week at the school tuck shop.

9

It follows that, short of accident or miscalculation, such as being born the fifteenth son of a ferret-handler in Thursoe, Littleton could scarcely fail to become an Etonian and, in the fullness of time, an Old Etonian.

The date of his birth also displayed that degree of ruthless calculation which was to mark his subsequent career. It ensured that, by the fateful year of 1939, Humphery would be eighteen years old and of military age. In the carrying out of this phase of his plans, Littelton received—and was ever quick to acknowledge in later life—invaluable assistance from the late Adolph Hitler, of whom it has been said. Herr Hitler used his not-inconsiderable influence to make it possible for the young Old Etonian to become a Guards Officer and an ex-Guards Officer within the short space of six years.

At least one authoritative history of World War Two* claims that by landing at the Salerno beach-head clutching a trumpet in his hand, Humphrey almost single-handed brought the Italian campaign to a successful conclusion. It is now thought that his role in the affair has perhaps been exaggerated and that his gallant and persistent trumpeting in the face of the enemy was responsible for fewer German casualties than at first claimed. Nevertheless, he was mentioned frequently in dispatches, leading eventually to his withdrawal from the Front and return to England. The scenes on VE Day, when the ex-Guards Officer designate was hoisted onto a handcart and towed, still trumpeting, through Piccadilly to the cheers of grateful Londoners, have been described in vivid detail by an eye-witness*.

Within months, Middleton, now a successful Old Etonian ex-Guards Officer, was poised for the most crucial phase in his career. It has been suggested by at least one base calumniator* that the road to becoming an Old Etonian ex-Guards Officer jazz trumpeter was a smooth one. It must be borne in mind that the Luttleton family, as it was originally spelt and often still is, goes back a long way into English history. The Luttletons were

10

sturdy cricketing folk much given to original and fascinating hobbies, and the pages of their family history** teem with Archbishop-cricketers, Cabinet Minister-cricketers, Public School Headmaster-cricketers and at least one Old Etonian Chief of the Imperial General Staff-cricketer.

With such a background, there was naturally enough considerable pressure upon young Humphrey to go into the family business. It should not be thought that he was ill-equipped for this. On the playing fields of Eton, he became noted as a fast-bowler of quite unparalleled velocity, trajectory and altitude, a distinction which for many years was marked by a commemorative metal plaque in the knee-joint of a Mr. Joby who recklessly sold sweets and soft drinks on the boundary immediately behind the bowler's arm.

It was in 1936 that Lyttelston made perhaps the most coolly-calculated move in the furtherance of his career, going with his mother during the Eton and Harrow cricket match at Lord's to buy his first trumpet, dressed in the full top-hat-silver-waistcoat-tail-coat regalia of the Eton First XI Supporters' Club. One half-hour lesson, a quick flip through the pages of the Nat Gonella Trumpet Tutor, a few hours' practice in the lavatory (now preserved for the nation) of his grandfather's house in London, and Hamphrey Lytteton was a trumpet player. But the battle was not yet won.

How near he came to becoming an Old Etonian ex-Guards Officer orchestral trumpeter, doomed to obscurity in the anonymous brass section of a symphony orchestra, can be judged from the words of Dr. Mervyn Bruxner, the conductor of the Eton School Orchestra, on hearing Humprey perform the Jeremiah Clark Trumpet Voluntary within a few weeks of taking up the instrument—'Good God!' One should mention, too, a later performance, arranged for trumpet, pipe organ and stentorian tenor voice, of the aria 'Sound an Alarm' from Handel's *Judas Maccabeus*, a musical event which is marked by a

11

commemorative metal plaque erected only recently at the approaches to Eton College which reads 'WINDSOR BRIDGE IS NOW CLOSED TO TRAFFIC DUE TO THE DISCOVERY OF A PERMANENT STRUCTURAL FAULT. NO ACCESS TO WINDSOR VIA ETON HIGH STREET'.

The manner in which Himphrey became an Old Etonian ex-Guards Officer jazz trumpeter is now too well-known to need reiteration. The names of historic stepping-stones—the Nuthouse, Regent Street . . . the Orange Tree, Friern Barnet . . . the Red Barn, Bexleyheath—are etched in the annals of jazz history*, not to mention his liver. The careful reader will note that as yet the infant Lutterworth's full ambition was unrealised. He had yet to become a *well-known* Old Etonian ex-Guards Officer jazz trumpeter. At this point he met up fortuitously with several people who were to have a considerable influence on his career.

One was Canadian-born jazz clarinetist Wally 'Trog' Fawkes, a member of George Webb's Dixielanders, who persuaded Hphmrey to join the band. Shortly afterwards, on the occasion of the first International Jazz Festival at Nice, Canadian-born *Daily Mail* temporary Foreign Correspondent W. E. Fawkes wrote an article for his paper revealing that the young trumpet-player from England who was appearing at the festival was, in fact, an Old Etonian ex-Guards Officer jazz trumpeter whose ancestor, Humphrey Lyttelton, had been an associate of Guy 'Trog' Fawkes in the Gunpowder Plot. Overnight Lyllelton had become well-known.

It wasn't long, however, before Lymington confided in friends that life at the top, as a well-known Old Etonian ex-Guards Officer jazz trumpeter, was far from easy. For one thing, there was the competition. Was not Old Stoic, ex-Navy author-scriptwriter-art critic blues-singer George Melly coming up fast behind him, becoming more well-known every minute. With a ruthless energy unusual in a man of his size (six-foot three in his stockinged feet, slightly smaller in shoes) he threw himself into the task of accumulating hyphens.

Within weeks, thanks to a broadcast on what was then the BBC Home Service entitled 'How I bought my first trumpet', he had become jazz trumpeter-broadcaster. Meeting up fortuitously with Canadian-born clarinetist-journalist-cartoonist 'Trog' of the *Daily Mail*, he became overnight a jazz-trumpeter-broadcaster-cartoonist. He started his own band with Canadian-born former George Webb Dixielander cartoonist-journalist-clarinetist Wally Fawkes, thus turning into a well-known Old Etonian ex-Guards Officer jazz trumpeter-broadcaster-cartoonist-bandleader.

There seemed no end to the man's achievements. The purchase of a pair of binoculars, a quick tour of fifty London restaurants, the acceptance of an article by *Punch*, an appearance on '*Any Questions?*' and a chat with Michael Parkinson led to his becoming, by 1975 a well-known Old Etonian ex-Guards Officer jazz trumpeter- broadcaster- cartoonist- bandleader-birdwatcher- gastronome- humorist- panellist- TV- personality. It was fantastic, incredible, unpreceden . . .

Enough! When the well-known Old Etonian- ex-Guards Officer- jazz trumpeter- broadcaster- cartoonist- bandleader-birdwatcher- gastronome- humorist- panelist- TV personality-corpse is finally laid to rest, let some professional obituarist in need of the gig put the finishing touches. I have given all the help I can and, in the process, outlined the patchwork quilt of a career, as yet only just begun, which this book may well turn out to be about.

* *I Play As I Please* by Humphrey Lyttelton (McGibbon & Kee, remaindered at 25p).

** Wisden's Almanack.

Warm Up

G.W.L

THERE'S A SUBTLE DISTINCTION between what you remember about your father and what you have learned. I know that George Lyttelton was a distinguished and inspired teacher of English literature at Eton, because many people, in all walks of life, who feel that he opened their eyes and ears to Shakespeare and Milton and Dickens have told me so. He wrote lengthy and superb letters to a vast number of recipients, contributed cricket reports to *The Times* and composed (in longhand and with laborious care) quite a number of articles, papers and essays which were published. He could not have been a journalist—it took him days to polish and rephrase a thousand-word piece in his elegant (and painstakingly-acquired) handwriting. His friends often tried to goad him into writing a book. I remember him once gnashing his teeth with genuine rage (distinguishable from the petrifying but often simulated fury which we knew as children) at the implication that he shied from authorship because of laziness. 'You blithering idiots!' he cried at the world at large, 'Does it not occur to you that I might not *want* to write a book?'

We didn't see much of him as small children, except on holidays. His study was on the second landing, a huge room full of books—from wall to ceiling on shelves, stacked in piles on every flat surface and moving like an invading army across the floor. Along the same landing, next to their bedroom, was his dressing-room, a place of some importance in our lives since the first step towards emancipation from nanny's rule was being allowed to have a bath downstairs in the dressing-room. This room I associate most closely with my father. It had a flowered carpet, a well-stacked bookshelf at one end, golf clubs and a cricket bat in the corner of the bookshelf, golf balls and tees, and, for no reason I ever discovered, a large bottle of vinegar on the huge mantelpiece, photos of old school and university friends, mostly in athletic postures, everywhere and, on the dressing table under a mirror on the wall, a bookrest on a pedestal so that he could read and memorise poetry while he shaved. There was also a distinctive bottle of hair-cream, of a brand to which he remained faithful throughout his life, which smelt 'like Father' and which, as I discovered after some furtive experiment, flattened one's hair back in congealed strands, solid as wire, and gave one a very grown-up look. The bath was the biggest in the world, and a sort of ottoman with a cork top had to be put up against it to enable us to climb in.

The introductory—and cursory—synopsis of his scholastic attainments is necessary to offset the memories I have of G.W.L., which are mostly lighthearted if not actually frivolous. In the family circle his sense of fun went back beyond the schoolboy stage to a sort of nursery innocence. He was scrupulous in not uttering rude words, even of a mild lavatorial kind, in the hearing of my mother and sisters. One morning at the time of the Korean war, he was reading his *Times* at the breakfast table when he was suddenly overtaken by convulsions. Pressed from all sides to share the joke, he resolutely refused until at last he agreed to write it on a piece of paper for my eyes alone. The note, carefully folded several times and passed down the table with much adjuration to secrecy, read 'THE SOUTH KOREAN DEPUTY PRIME MINISTER'S NAME IS MR. BUM SUK LEE'.

18

At meals, especially when all the family were together on holiday, he was by any nursery standards badly behaved. I'm talking now of when he was about fifty and the oldest of us were just entering our teens. One might have expected a revered schoolmaster of awesome repute to have brought a certain restrained dignity to the dinner-table. One of his favourite games, in which everyone but my mother joined enthusiastically, was to beat a rhythmic tattoo in 6/8 time on the table—da-dum da-dum, da-di-di-di-dum—starting very stealthily and then getting louder and louder until the cutlery and glasses jumped about. If asked to pass anything like a bread roll or an orange, he would ask 'Tunnicliffe or Denton?' and withhold it until he got an answer. This was a Lyttelton family joke. Tunnicliffe and Denton were cricketers, one famous for his slip-catches, the other renowned for his work in the deep-field. I don't recall which was which, but if you were lucky enough to nominate the deep-fielder, the object would be lobbed over gently. The wrong choice brought it thudding into your chest or, more often, ricocheting round the room.

I should say here that outbreaks like this were strictly rationed and were offset at other times by a profound, but no less entertaining, pessimism. He had little fragments of song which would suddenly pop up during lulls in the conversation—one of the jolliest began 'Born one day when his mother was away . . .' and ended 'No wonder Little Billy Blunder went stark, staring mad!' More often he would intone, in a sepulchral voice, a sombre ditty that went—'Days and moments quickly flying . . . blend the living with the dead . . . soon will you and I be lying . . . each within his narrow bed.'

It may be that my own invincible optimism derives from a youthful observation that few, if any, of his gloomy prognostications ever came to the sort of fulfilment that he expected. 'I suppose you all realise,' he announced one lunchtime in the late 'thirties, 'that in five years time I shall be unable to move a

19

muscle, with the possible exception of my eyeballs.' He was in his middle fifties then, and despite a rheumatic disease which slowed him up a bit, he remained active enough to fall out of a tree at sixty-seven, get knocked off his bike by a careless motor-cyclist at seventy-two and be jolted off the top of a bus when not far short of eighty. Whenever we talked of doing something 'next year' he would add in a voice of doom '. . . if there *is* a next year'. Yet the years came and went without one, so far as I recollect, ever being cancelled.

Short of a recurrence of the Flood, the thing he dreaded most was a Run On The Pound. We had an Impending Financial Crisis in our house long before anyone else even began to suspect that there was something wrong, and I grew up in the belief that the fall of a couple of notches in the exchange rate of the pound brought the workhouse several streets nearer. Today I can look back with equanimity on a succession of runs on the pound which amount to nothing less than monetary diarrhoea, and the only time it ever had a noticeable affect on me was when a fee contracted in Deutschmarks for an engagement in Germany suddenly inflated behind my back.

It would be grotesque to use the word 'pig' in respect of one as sensitive and, despite his huge frame, graceful as my father. But I suppose he was, by today's stern standards, a male chauvinist. In the old Eton days there were servants. When he and my mother moved to Suffolk after his retirement, he quite enjoyed doing, not the actual washing-up, but the drying-up afterwards. He took it very seriously, completely reorganising the box in which the knives and forks were kept and making, we thought, rather a fuss if someone put a small fork where a large fork should go.

He was no cook. By this I mean not that he didn't cook well, but that he didn't cook *anything*. From the cradle, his upbringing was founded on one unshakable article of faith—that God would provide, not only food, but someone to cook it.

20

Only once in his life did he have reason to doubt this. It was after they moved to Suffolk, where my mother cooked breakfast and supper and a daily help took care of the midday meal. Once my mother went away on a short visit without him, having carefully arranged things so that he would only have to get himself breakfast. As he was quite happy with nothing more than a bowl of porridge, there seemed to be no problem. Before she went, she wrote out, in words of one syllable, instructions on how to make overnight porridge—how much oatmeal and water to put in the casserole, which oven to leave it in till morning.

When he came to interpret these instructions, a thought occurred to him. What possible reason could there be, other than a characteristically feminine awe of convention, for making the porridge in a casserole and then decanting it into a soup plate? Chuckling, no doubt, at the illogicality of women and their capacity for making work, he put a handful of oats straight into the soup plate, added water and put it uncovered into the oven. Next morning, he discovered that he had invented an oat-cake—no delicacy, it must be admitted, but compact and quite suitable as hard, not to say indestructible, rations for a polar expedition.

When it came to food, he was a man of simple tastes, although my mother always regarded with deep scepticism his oft-repeated avowal that 'bread and cheese will do me perfectly well'. She noted that whenever she provided some alternative to bread and cheese—a steak and kidney pie, say, with two veg. and apple pie with thick cream to follow—he attacked it with all the enthusiasm of a man who has just been rescued after six months on a barren island. But it's true to say that he didn't go very much for rich and alcoholic feasting. I remember the day he came back from having lunch with a relation who was a tycoon of global, if not cosmic, influence. He always dreaded these occasions, being a man of measured habits

21

whose curriculum made no allowances for the crippling midday meal or the recuperative afternoon nap.

On the day in question, he was immensely relieved when the tycoon, pleading pressure of appointments on which, it appeared, the future of the world hung, announced at the outset that they would have to eat a truncated meal in his office instead of going out. Waving aside the apologies with genuine unconcern, my father relaxed in the comforting expectation of a cheese sandwich—with some pickle, perhaps—brought in by a panting office-boy.

Some minutes later, an official looking disturbingly like a butler insinuated himself into the room and passed to the captain of industry a murmured message. To my father eavesdropping uneasily on the other side of the huge executive desk, it seemed to convey the dreaded information that luncheon was served. Gliding across the opulent carpet, the official then flung open two sleekly-panelled doors to reveal, in the adjoining room, a vast boardroom table bow-legged under the weight of food. To use my father's own awe-struck words, there were acres of caviare, smoked salmon, game pie and mousse, picketed by magnums of champagne and decanters of port. That night, home again, he sat in his armchair trying to read, breathing more heavily than usual and occasionally giving a convulsive shudder at the thought of what he would have had to put away had not the critical state of international high finance demanded a snack in the office.

As the second son of a ninth viscount, he had considerable experience of meals in stately homes. When I look back myself to childhood holidays spent with innumerable cousins at Babraham Hall or Longford Castle, my first memory is of sitting at a huge dining-room table at lunch, watching with some awe as a human conveyor belt of maids and footmen brought course after course to the table. I can see my father sitting opposite, massively polite but revealing mounting impatience through the movement of his eyebrows. They were superb eyebrows—bristling reddish antennae set at a downward sloping angle, capable of beetling prodigiously but at their most eloquent when they began moving up his huge brow through degrees ranging from surprise to utter disbelief at the folly of mankind.

He always liked to be out and about on holidays and, in the country, was a great one for lopping, sawing and otherwise maiming trees. As lunch dragged on towards three o'clock with no apparent slackening in the flow of food to the table, the eyebrows would reach full stretch as though about to take off and go flapping away through the window in an independent bid for freedom. On one memorable occasion he took direct action, though he always protested afterwards that it was an accident. Near the end of one gastronomic marathon, a colossal bunch of grapes was carried round, its great weight supported by a curved silver bracket from which also hung a pair of embossed scissors. When it reached him on its imperial passage round the table, he took the scissors and applied them with all the delicate precision of an operating surgeon to one of the stalks. As it happens, it was the main stalk, and with one snip the whole massive bunch fell to the floor with a moist thud, leaving three or four grapes suspended rather foolishly from the bracket. In the ensuing confusion, with his family and nephews and nieces unable to contain themselves, a motion to adjourn the meal was carried without a vote.

I have one curious trait which I believe to be inherited from my father and which may explain his lack of stamina at formal affairs. Whenever ten or more people are gathered together in one room, chattering away like broiler-fowl at feeding-time, I go deaf. It is as if the input channels of my ears become overloaded and automatically cut out as a precaution against short-circuiting and bursting into flames. For me, social convocations for drinks or meals turn, when warmed up and under way, into surrealistic happenings in which lips move, tongues

23

G.W.L. invents an OATCAKE

wag, eyebrows plunge and soar but nothing that could remotely be described as human speech reaches me.

At family gatherings, when questions, answers, anecdotes and reminiscences were crossing at all angles like a conversational Crewe Junction, my father often betrayed the symptoms. His face would assume a bland, withdrawn expression and he would start talking to the dog, a sure sign that, for the moment, human intercourse had become impracticable. On one startling occasion, he was brought back into the conversation by a question about the weather they had been having in East Anglia. 'Mrs. who?' was his discouraging response.

I remember him telling me once about an MCC lunch which he attended with his cousin and great friend, Father Ted Talbot of the Mirfield Brotherhood of the Resurrection. My father often made after-dinner speeches at the MCC. All we at home knew of the events was when he returned with his breast pocket stuffed with cigars which he had scooped with his great shovel of a hand out of the box that circulated at the end of the meal. He rarely smoked them himself, but they came in handy for guests. At the lunch in question, he and Ted Talbot sat next to each other. Halfway through the meal, he bellowed into the reverend ear that he had never in his life heard such a hubbub of conversation. Father Talbot in turn put his mouth to my father's ear and suggested that they should try a simple experiment. If they burst into song, how long would it be before they were detected? Thereupon the two of them, towering, bespectacled schoolmaster and craggy, befrocked cleric, began to sing, 'O God, Our Help In Ages Past . . .', *mezzo forte* and *con spirito*. They got through three verses quite unnoticed before they collapsed in unseemly giggles.

Most of the enduring things I learnt from my father were by example rather than precept. His 'serious talk' with me as I approached puberty lingers in my mind solely for its almost startling brevity. He was standing in the traditional position with his back to the fireplace and he uttered the injunction in a strong, resonant voice with a stern lowering of the massive eyebrows, as if to make up in portentousness what his message lacked in length and detail. 'Eschew evil!' he boomed, then gave me a heavy paternal bang on the shoulder and left the room, humming to himself.

Mucking About

MY GREATEST ACHIEVEMENT at school was to bring aimless leisure to a fine art. That I had a talent for it was clear much earlier in life. Some time ago I discovered, among the family junk, a diary which I had kept for a day or two as a small boy. It hinted at a richly enjoyable childhood.

> Friday. In morning, mucked about. Had lunch, then went for a walk. Afterwards, mucked about.
>
> Saturday. Got up late. Played cricket but we lost the ball, so mucked about.
>
> Sunday. Mucked about.

My diary is reticent about the actual details, but I remember quite well that mucking about involved a wealth of genuinely idle activity—throwing pebbles at tin cans, counting up to a thousand, tying useless knots in string, dangling the feet in the lily pond, riding a bike in diminishing circles until you fell over, seeing who could spit farthest and spying furtively on total strangers as they walked past the front gate.

Child psychologists—spoilsports by definition—now tell us that what we called mucking about was really meaningful activity, an important phase in 'learning about life'. Piffle! If that were so, we would have learnt in one sharp practical lesson in elementary physics that riding a bicycle in too tight a circle

27

brings gravity into play with painful results, and we would have avoided it in future. But we didn't. We picked ourselves up and did it again and again, roaring with laughter.

The fact which we knew and the child psychologists still don't is that total idleness, claiming no function, bearing no fruit, serving no purpose, is wholly therapeutic and, what's more, jolly good for you. This of course runs quite counter to the Public School ethos into which I was plunged at the age of twelve. In public schools, it was (and perhaps still is) believed that a good game of cricket diverts natural urges which might otherwise lead to nameless malpractices behind the pavilion. I have always considered cricket to be a curiously inappropriate sport for this purpose. In my brief experience of the game, it involved seemingly endless periods of such acute boredom and inactivity that a saint of unsullied purity of mind would be tempted to nip round the back of the pavilion for a quick malpractice out of sheer desperation.

I also had to contend with the theory that violence and assault, not to say murder, on the field of sport dispel aggression which might without it be directed towards lynching the masters or toasting small boys over the fire. At my old school, they have a traditional spectacle called the Wall Game which must have been specially designed to fulfil this purpose, combining as it does the merits of rugger, soccer, boxing, tag wrestling, weight-lifting and open-cast mining. It's essentially a low budget sport—all you need is a wall, a ball and a strip of mud.

Actually, the ball is expendable, as my father in his Eton days discovered one afternoon when things were a bit quiet in the middle of the scrum (they call it a 'bully', which figures). By the way of a scientific experiment, he scooped a deep hole in the mud, put the ball in it and shovelled and patted the mud back into place. He then set about making the sort of encouraging noises appropriate to a player in possession. 'Heave up, you chaps! . . . We're gaining ground on the rotters! . . . Pass it back, Wynnington-Smythe, you duffer!' The great human mass went on heaving and pummelling and grunting heroically. They were still at it when the whistle blew for time. And the contestants went trotting off to their baths and their high tea without a backward glance at the tell-tale mound in mid-field.

With the ball playing such a negligible part in the proceedings, it's hardly necessary to have any rules, which is just as well since it is not every referee, lying flat on his face to insert the ball in the bully for kick-off, who manages to extricate himself in time.

After the game had been established for several centuries, it was found necessary to insist that those whose ears and temples were in constant abrasive contact with the wall should wear a thickly padded headpiece, to protect the brickwork. And at some stage there grew up a sort of gentleman's agreement that, while it is quite legal to knead, squash, knuckle and generally rearrange the face of the opponent nearest to you in order to weaken his resolve and his foothold in the mud, eye-gouging is bad form.

At six-foot-three and thirteen stone I was too small to play the Wall Game, and I got out of a lot of cricket by bribing the scorer to put me down as 8 not out—through which I achieved a reputation, not for skill, but for commendable consistence. This left plenty of time for mucking about, to which I set myself with a will.

I always used to think then that, in later life, mucking about would come very much more easily. How wrong I was. The achievement of idleness has been a constant struggle, straining ingenuity to its utmost.

The Yoga people have been on to this for years and have come up with some rather snappy little ideas. There's no end to the maddening duties and meaningful activities that can be got out of by squatting in a corner with your feet wrapped round the back of your neck. Unfortunately they spoil it all by harnessing it to some Grand Purpose, the achievement of something-or-other. The true mucker-about, the man entitled to the letters MA after his name, will have none of that. Having got his feet round his neck, he will see how far he can hop across the room on his haunches without giggling or will just stay there, propped against the wainscoting like a human rucksack, while his mind goes off on some irrelevant daydream.

The trouble with that kind of thing is that it presupposes that no one will interrupt the reverie with 'Haven't you fixed that washer yet?' or 'When's supper?' An acquaintance of mine of some years ago, who was married to one of nature's sergeant-majors, devised a splendid scheme with the telephone. At the first appearance of a cup to be washed up or a loose doorhandle to be fixed he would dash for the phone, mumbling something about promising to ring so-and-so. He then dialled the weather report (TIM would do, though it's difficult to explain away those pips) and engaged it in an urgent business conversation, sporadically holding the mouthpiece away from the ear to enable the suspicious listener to hear a voice at the other end, but not long enough to reveal that the voice was droning on about the temperature on the Air Ministry roof. Since the GPO inconsiderately employ golden-voiced ladies for these telephone services, the whole affair ended in divorce anyway, but it was a great idea at the time. The scheme had a dual-purpose— it got him off work and at the same time allowed him to indulge limitless fantasies about being a business tycoon. Furthermore, by ending the conversation with 'Right—I'll get down to that right away!' in a loud voice, he gave himself the cue to hurry away to his den with a harrassed expression, there to sit making chains out of paper-clips or colouring in the lettering on his cheque book with multi-coloured felt pens to his heart's content.

To get out of such arch-enemies of adult mucking-about as Do It Yourself, I have devised a ploy of my own. It's called Do It

To Yourself and works on the principle of the old wartime self-inflicted wound. It's main advantage is that it is simple—there is practically no commodity on sale in the handyman shops which cannot be used by the beginner to put himself out of effective DIY action for days. And you are talking to a man who has practically amputated a finger with *sandpaper*. The drawback to DITY, apart from the pain involved, is its tendency to generate a guilt complex. We call it the *Journey's End* syndrome—cowardice in the face of the enemy, letting down King and Country, the white feather, face slapped by patriotic ladies in Hyde Park, cut by friends in Bond Street, Mater crying, Pater resigning from all his clubs.

For the faint-hearted there is an alternative, and it's sabotage.

For Xmas a few years ago my wife Jill gave me a power-drill. 'A man and his Black and Decker . . .' the TV advert used to intone, showing a lantern-jawed he-man of the outer suburbs advancing, power-drill jutting menacingly at the hip, upon some quaking piece of home-repair. A power-drill spells death to mucking about. It becomes impossible to sit gazing idly into space without the eye alighting and focusing reluctantly upon some defect in the domestic environment which could be put right immediately by the simple expedient of boring a neat hole.

So there I am on the following Good Friday, all set for a muck-about of almost religious proportions, when the insidious thought intrudes that a batten screwed to the wall over the oven wouldn't half be useful. It is the work of a moment to assemble the power drill, plug in, switch on and commence drilling a neat hole right through the middle of the oven cable. One minute the drill is biting smoothly into the masonry under the firm but sensitive grip of a master craftsman, the next there is a blue flash, a small explosion, and in place of the rampant Tungsten Carbide Tipped Masonry Drill No. 8, a remnant of scorched

31

metal droops impotently. With the shops shut till Tuesday, ten tons of frozen provisions in the 'fridge and a severed electrical artery buried beyond reach of Do It Yourself in the walls, the inner and outer voices in favour of Dad getting down to some useful jobs over the holiday were instantly stifled.

Of course that sort of thing costs money and can lead to bad feeling. I learned from my dad the simplest way to achieve idleness, although as a man who was always up to something purposeful—reading, writing, taking exercise—he would have been horrified to know it. I call it the intellectual or philosophical ploy. All it needs is the discovery of a resounding word or phrase to endow idleness with a moral veneer. My father was a literary man who knew where to go for the right high-sounding quotation—or how, if all else failed, to invent one for himself. Every Sunday morning on holiday, my mother would enquire if he was going to accompany her to church. 'This morning,' he would say, avoiding an outright negative, 'I shall worship in the vast cathedral of immensity.' In his case it meant the golf course, but it could have covered any kind of al fresco mucking about.

My own word is 'gestating' and it's a lulu. 'I thought you said you had to go and work' say importunate members of my family when they catch me doodling floral patterns on the back of the telephone directory. 'I'm gestating,' I reply, and there's no answer to it. It need not only apply to creative work. All the best Do It Yourself books advise 'thinking the job through' before actually putting hand to chisel or paint brush. Don't rush into it, they warn. Catch me, say I, settling down surrounded by tools and impedimenta to a good gestate. In fact, the only reason I've digressed on this subject is for the gestation it afforded. And when I tell you that in the process I broke my own record—eleven wine-corks perfectly balanced on top of each other and resisting the destructive breeze for all of thirty-eight seconds—you have to agree it's been well worth it.

Mucker-about of high achievement I may be, but as a family man I've never had much success with holidays. I've tried. I have chased toddlers all over Heathrow departure lounge, nursed nippers through seasickness, trekked overland with what has seemed like a car-load of monkeys.

'Lyttelton,' my old staff sergeant in the army used to say, 'you'll never make a soldier—no method, no method at all.' Well, I fancy he would think again if he could have seen me back in the Sixties marshalling the family for our annual visit to North Wales. Each year was more impressive. 'Make your plan and stick to it' was one maxim that lodged in my subconscious at some stage in my officer training. With this in my mind I always informed the troo . . . sorry, the family, that we would mobilise promptly at 1000 hrs on the Tuesday. A cynic watching us trundle off down the drive at precisely 1147 hrs on the Wednesday might say that my plan had misfired. I can tell him that it was thanks to my clear and decisive battle orders that we got off before the week-end. As my wife used to say in tones which came perilously close to mutiny, packing for five people for a fortnight in a place where sunny spells, sea mists, snow, heatwave, hail, hurricane and humidity can all occur in one day, and usually do, is no pushover and I ought to try it one day.

I always left out of my reckoning, too, the inexorable way in which toys which had lain dormant in the remote recesses of cupboards for years suddenly became indispensable items of the children's equipment. In the back of my mind, I suppose, was the thrust from Battipaglia to Salerno in '43 when, under my supervision as signals officer of the 6th Battalion, Grenadier Guards, the signals truck was packed full of diverse equipment with a jigsaw precision that left the inspecting C.O. speechless—a phenomenon which cannot be attributed entirely to his discovery that the batteries for the signalling lamps had been left behind.

It was with something of the same feeling of pride that I surveyed the neatly stacked car boot at zero hour (amended) minus two, only to see it disrupted by the last-minute and apparently urgent inclusion of roller skates, a headless Teddy Bear in the throes of a sawdustectomy, two plastic walkie-talkie sets minus batteries (ah! shades of Salerno!), a battered box of Monopoly distributing counterfeit largesse in all directions, several cameras with vital spools missing, a lidless tin full of broken crayons and clogged pencil-sharpeners, an ill-assorted rabble of plastic animals that would have given Noah hysterics and innumerable inflatable rubber objects with their stoppers missing. At one stage in the packing process I was tempted to resort to one of the more ghastly clichés of authority by crying 'If you play ball with me, I'll play ball with you!', foreseeing in the nick of time that it would be taken literally with whoops of delight and further loss of time.

It became a matter of tradition that, every year, we packed the car and travelled to Wales in relentless rain. This made planning and foresight all the more essential. One year an improvised tarpaulin with which I covered the roofrack leaked and driving rain infiltrated a suitcase, transferring the Caribbean motif of a rather snazzy beachshirt of mine on to all my plain shirts, vests, pants and even pyjamas. To this day, the local residents of Harlech know me as the man who anticipated the Flower People by several years. After that, of course, my tarpaulin drill was impeccable. We used to have one of those 'spiders' with elastic tentacles that stretch over the luggage and sometimes release their hold and smash your glasses while you're taking the strain. On one trip some dozy individual (no, of course it wasn't me!) stuck the hooks *through* the tarpaulin, weakening it it in the face of a stiff headwind. Still, I think my old staff sergeant would have been proud to see us thundering off up the M1, no more than twenty-six hours behind schedule, with great fronds of tarpaulin flying like proud pennants behind us.

I am as non-violent and pacifist as the next man, but there's something about a seaside holiday that never fails to rekindle a dormant bellicosity. Perhaps it's the sight, at breakfast-time, of the rival armies making their plans and dispositions, thermos-flasks at the ready, maps unfurled and propped against the marmalade pots. It may be the routine of the nightly briefing in the TV lounge, when the rival commanders make their silent Appreciation of the Situation while the briefing officer at the London Weather Centre warns of deep depressions advancing from the west and cold fronts holding static positions on a line from North East Scotland to the Wash. Certainly no man with red blood in his veins can fail to shiver with the thrill of battle when, advancing upon the beach, he hears from his advance scouts the sudden challenging cry 'Mum! Dad! There's some-body sitting in OUR PLACE!!!'

It throws a revealing light on man's chronic inability to live at peace with his neighbour that, given a beach large enough to provide perfectly adequate *lebensraum* for everyone, some ruth-less aggressor will always plant himself and his barbaric family on the one spot which by tradition, pride of place, Squatters' Rights and sheer, straightforward justice, clearly belongs to you. Of course, seasoned campaigners will not be unprepared for this eventuality. In my experience, the most effective weapon for dislodging an enemy from prepared positions is a baby, preferably one that has reached the crawling stage. No giant tank was ever built more impregnable and unstoppable than a baby hell-bent on appropriating a bucket and spade or demolishing a sand-castle. All you have to do is point it in the right direction and let go.

I realise that it is not every family that can rustle up a baby at short notice, and there are very effective alternatives—a small boy with a plunging kite, for instance, or a roving dog that has been sedulously trained throughout the winter to cock its leg against anything that looks like a gaily-coloured canvas windshield. I must confess to reservations about the latter. It should perhaps be kept in reserve for an enemy who blatantly defies the Geneva convention by opening up with a transistor radio, say, or sending ingratiating children to establish a Fifth Column in your midst.

Of course, not all of your problems will stem from an external enemy. There is the question of man-management, of controlling and inspiring your own troops. In this respect, perhaps I might underline a basic principle with a cautionary tale from my own experience. It was as a newly-fledged second-lieutenant at Victoria Barracks, Windsor, that I learnt, in an initiation lecture, never to qualify or explain an order. It only invites argument and tempts disobedience. What I should have said to my daughter Georgina was 'Come out of the sea now . . . why? . . . because I say so!' It might have earned me a look of dumb insolence and a black mark from Dr. Spock, but it would have achieved results. What I actually said was '. . . because your teeth are chattering'—and back came the answer like a boomerang . . . 'Oh, that's all right—only my teeth are cold!'

We started going to Wales after a series of family holidays abroad from which we returned physically shattered and mentally in urgent need of a rest-cure. They were so fraught with calamity that, to turn disappointment into fulfilment, failure into success, I started to keep a holiday diary. I don't mean one of your 'Arrived 3 p.m. . . . unpacked . . . weather good . . .' telegraphic affairs, but a full, comprehensive chronicle of events.

You have to admit it's good thinking. For the price of a solid notebook and a reliable ball-point, you are transformed from the helpless victim of circumstances into one who preys upon them. You have become, in the very literal sense, a journalist, eager to be where the action is and hungry for copy. From now on, the plane that arrives uneventfully on time, the hotel that lives up to the brochure's Utopian promise, the weather that furnishes a backdrop of unremitting blue sky and sunshine—these all become items on the debit side of a holiday, boring and undiaryworthy non-events.

This is no idle theory. The best holiday abroad we ever had, in Italy in 1963, was, brochure-wise, a ghastly failure. The holiday villa in a quiet seaside resort turned out to be a grimy slum separated from the sea by a lethal main road and fifty yards away from an all-night discotheque. The 'own kitchen and refrigerator' were in fact used as overflows by the Italian matriarch who owned the place, as I discovered on the first morning when, fuddled with sleep but feeling that breakfast in bed might restrain my wife and family from going home by the earliest plane, I reached blearily into the fridge for some bacon and withdrew a cold and clammy cockerel's head.

At this point I should say that my own holiday diaries have been blessed by what I can only call a jinx where weather is concerned. I sometimes wonder why I have never put it to commercial use. If frost and hail were deemed necessary over the Sahara desert, it would only require me, plus deck-chair, swimming trunks and a small bottle of sun-oil, to bring it about. The only time I ever went to the south of France in the spring, Nice had an unprecedented fall of snow.

Italy in 1963 ran true to form. Thunderstorms rent the air, causing among other diversions a spectacular short-circuit in our slum's naked wiring system. Despite our landlady's promises, hedged with oaths, threats and imprecations, that the famed 'sole Italiano' would inevitably burst upon us in its full glory within a matter of hours, all we glimpsed all week was an anaemic and watery fried-egg in the sky. And the sea! Rebelling, I presume, against its tedious reputation as a warm and azure summer mill-pond, the Mediterranean heaved and threshed and thundered, turning an ugly, vengeful greeny-grey in the process.

Our suntans may have languished but our diary thrived. One

thing we found out quite early on was that the English—that great seafaring race—are famous, in vulgar Italian seaside resorts, for getting drowned. It was in vain that we explained to giggling foreigners that the red flags flapping over the beach as a warning to the timid and the craven struck the intrepid English as a challenge to that authority over the sea which is our island heritage. And we had plenty of opportunity to explain, since scarcely a day went by without a stir of excitement and the sudden massing of ant-like figures at the sea's edge far along the beach announcing that another Inglese had been fished, limp and gasping, from the deep.

Inevitably, and to the unutterable joy of one eager diarist, it happened on our beach. Well, actually it happened on the beach next door. The whole shore line was divided into strips like medieval smallholdings, and each strip had its own deckchair concessionaires and life-saving team of beach boys with strictly defined administrative boundaries. When through the howling wind a cry of 'HELP!' was heard, as commanding and phlegmatic and English as the cry of 'TAXI!' in Mayfair, it could be seen that the head bobbing about in the swell a little way out to sea was located within the sphere of influence of the beach next door. But their four-man rescue team, making a frontal attack on the waves, couldn't launch their catamaran—the sea just up-ended it and threw it back over their heads.

It was after the fourth attempt, when the cry for help began to take on a note of impatience, that our team decided to defy protocol and intervene. When not fishing Englishmen out of the drink they used to play endless games of beach football, calling each others' names incessantly. So we felt some pride of acquaintanceship as we watched them run down to the sea's edge, catamaran at the shoulder. Mario, Toni, Pierino and Blotto (all right, so it couldn't have been, but there's no time to go into that now. A man's life is at stake!)—all good men and true. Launching at an oblique angle to the waves, they had better luck than their rivals (for rivals they had become) and were soon afloat and on their way, paddling and shouting simultaneously.

If your holidays have been plagued by good weather and you have never seen an Italian rescue at sea, you might feel that the excitement is now over. A deft hoist, the triumphant return of rescuers and rescued, and that's it. That, my friends, was very far from it. As soon as the first team of rescuers saw their rivals encroaching on their territory, they hurled away their catamaran with shouts of disgust and frustration and dived, still shouting, into the waves to swim for it. Meanwhile Mario, Toni, Pierino and Blotto had reached the drowning man. Pierino, leaning over impulsively to grab the Englishman's arm, almost overturned the craft. Mario, who seemed to be the team's skipper, hit him with a paddle and he let go. An altercation ensued, clearly audible from the shore, during which the catamaran drifted several yards away from the now flailing suppliant. Toni must have been responsible for navigation for, on seeing what had happened, Pierino hit him. While he floundered in the bottom of the boat, the other three paddled furiously and soon, with some desperate scrabbling in the ocean, the Englishman was grasped, hoisted aboard and thrown with total lack of ceremony on to the deck.

Turning for home the rescuers met the first of the swimmers who, eager no doubt to lay some claim to the salvage, grabbed the bows of the catamaran as if to tow it. Toni hit him. The swimmer and his fellows then retreated and made for shallow water, where they turned and waited while the sea, no respecter of territories, swept the enemy towards their beach. As they paddled out to try and grab the craft, Mario, Toni, Pierino and Blotto hit them. An epic free fight broke out in the shallows.

In the midst of it all, the rescued Inglese, who had now recovered his breath and his *sang froid*, climbed off the boat and waded ashore unnoticed, to be accorded a dramatic and tearful sailor-home-from-the-sea welcome by his wife. Being, as I think

I mentioned, an Englishman, he was not a man to just walk off without doing the right thing. When the fighting subsided, he walked across to Blotto, who was nearest to him, and extended his hand in a magnanimous gesture, his face radiating gratitude. Blotto hit it.

Now, own up. You don't get a story like that just sitting about in the sun, do you?

Happily, it fell to me to restore some vestige of our national dignity by carrying out a rescue at sea myself. At high tide and on a calm day, one could wade out from the beach, swim a few strokes across a dip and reach a broad ledge where the shallow water was warm and clear. Occupying the villa below us was an Italian couple, the wife pear-shaped and timid, the husband suggesting by his pallid torso and tendency to go into a crabby handstand whenever anyone was watching that he was a sedentary worker of athletic aspiration rather than achievement.

One afternoon on the beach, he persuaded his wife, who couldn't swim, to let him carry her on his shoulders across to the ridge. She was reluctant, he was noisily confident. It was only when he walked steeply down into the sea and disappeared from view that he realised, too late, that the whole enterprise was based on a miscalculation. Feeling the water lapping around her knees, the wife began to scream, at the same time tightening her grip on the man's head by clasping his nose.

I was returning to the shore at a stately breast-stroke when the momentary appearance of the man's face, purple and with the bulging eyes flashing mute distress signals, caused me to alter course and steam to the rescue. Having with some firmness prised the woman from her husband's head, it was simple to steer her, now limp and buoyant, to the safety of land.

As sea rescues go, it was unspectacular. But it was something, in the prevailing circumstances, for an Englishman to have prevented an excitable Italian lady from drowning her husband in six feet of water, and I still feel that, before castigat-

Sole Italiano

Rescue at Sea

ing her loudly for her lack of co-operation, he could have said thanks. It would have given me the chance to hit him.

Back at the villa, life provided endless diary-fodder. The owner of the villa was an excitable lady of Franco-Italian origin with one of those hoarse, stentorian voices that seem to have lost all intermediate modulations between a shout and a whisper. We complained to her on the second day that the bathroom cistern had a leak which baptised the sedentary occupant of the loo with a steady drip on the crown of the head. She informed us—and everyone else within a five-mile radius—that it would get no worse if we didn't pull the chain and that her husband, then working on the railways in Switzerland, would be home on leave shortly to see to it. We bought a plastic bucket which was kept full of water in the bath for flushing the loo, and waited for the husband to arrive.

Ten days later, returning from the beach, we were met by a landlady speechless with excitement. She dragged us to the bathroom and, panting for breath, pointed triumphantly at the cistern, which dripped no longer. We gathered that the husband had been and gone, finding time in the fleeting moments of conjugal reunion to perform this minor miracle.

It was when somebody later in the evening tried to pull the chain that we found out how he had done it. Borrowing our bucket to mix two gallons of cement, he had poured the lot into the cistern, solidifying every moving part and, in passing, plugging the tiny hole. We had to hoist our landlady on to the seat to convince her what her handyman had done, and her rage was terrible to witness. She hurried downstairs to her own apartments and re-emerged minutes later with a mallet and a vast chisel. Throughout our evening meal the sounds of demolition came from the bathroom. Eventually she appeared, purple in the face, to indicate that the status quo had been restored. It had, except that the drip was now a deluge.

A couple of years later, after a holiday in Spain which had not even the saving grace of comedy, we chose Portugal and I took elaborate precautions. By good luck, I had some work in Portugal earlier in the year, and I visited the little fishing village we had chosen to reassure myself—and my family—that it was everything the brochure claimed. I noted the blissful quietness, the quality of the local food, the almost Scandinavian scrupulousness of the sanitary arrangements. This last was especially important. In Italy we had been persecuted by that temperamental lavatory cistern, in Spain, the water supply had failed whenever it rained, a perversion of the normal provisions of Nature which I never fathomed. When I got home from my working visit, I was able to cheer everyone up with my report. I should have been warned perhaps by the fact that, while they sing incessantly about April in Portugal, there is a certain reticence about August in Portugal. On the coach from Lisbon airport to our hotel, the lady courier broke the news that, owing to an unprecedented drought, the water in the village would be cut off from noon until seven-thirty the following morning, and we would be wise to fill the bath before going out for the day. It was a situation rich in dramatic possibilities, most of which came to fruition in an astonishingly short time. On the very first night, a friend with whom we were to spend the holiday returned to his room after a long session at the bar and, in his efforts not to disturb his wife, slipped in his stockinged feet and sat fully clothed in the bath. A few mornings later, I was roused from a deep sleep by an agitated knocking on my door. I opened an eye in time to see one of my slippers float past on a swift current, rounding an island of sodden underwear with a navigational instinct I had never suspected. The floor was two inches deep in water, and the knocking on the door was by the lady from the room below who had begun to take the overflow. Fortunately, she had previously made the same mistake, forgetting to ensure, before she went to bed, that the bath taps were turned off. She even helped me mop up with bath-towels.

These were routine enough occurrences. What was totally unpredictable was the trick cyclist on a tight wire who was established through the holiday season on a bit of bare ground across the road from our hotel—and our bedroom window— every night. His act, which we never actually saw but which we could follow from the hysterical commentary even under a defensive screen of four pillows, consisted of riding on a two-stroke motor cycle up a tight wire stretched at a gradient of about one-in-four. As he revved and goaded his machine, every inch of his progress was described with mounting excitement by the commentator over the tannoy. At the height of the din, there was a triumphant cry of 'Viva Portugal!' and an ear-splitting national anthem. Reaching the top, the rider had dexterously unfurled the Portuguese flag.

Hanging About

FROM ADOLESCENCE to the present day, I have spent quite a lot of time pondering on what I am going to be when I grow up.

When I was about sixteen, there was a plan afoot in my family to put me into shipping. It was a notion born of desperation. Some years before, while still at private school, I had gone through a nautical phase, sparked off by a guided tour over the luxury liner *Olympic*, in dry-dock at Southampton. Fired fleetingly with the spirit of Drake and Nelson, I took home all the give-away leaflets and subsequently wrote off in all directions for brochures. The literature about world tours which arrived in due course, hopefully addressed 'Dear Mr. Lyttelton', soon assuaged my wanderlust. When you've seen one wide-angle photo of an empty luxury dining-room, you've seen them all, and I went on to film stars, whose photos showed slightly more variety.

When the question of a career arose, this passing interest in seafaring, though a thing of the past, was nonetheless a straw at which my parents clutched eagerly. Through a relative in the City, an introduction was arranged with a big shipping magnate. My father and I went to have lunch with him at Simpson's-in-the-Strand, just the place for momentous, man-to-man decisions.

Sir John talked about shipping and its multiplicity of drawbacks for a young man in search of a career. My father listened with all the interest he could muster, showing, as the talk of clerking, overseas postings and promotional prospects unfolded, intense relief that it was my career and not his that was under discussion. And I just sat, revealing, I suspect, rather less animation than the great carcasses of meat that trundled past under their silver domes.

The point came when Sir John was interrupted in the middle of a long anecdote by the arrival of the cheese trolley. He seemed very particular about the condition of his cheese and took some time selecting not only his own portion but ours as well. At the end of this prolonged hiatus, he turned to my father and said 'Now then, where was I?' My father looked blank for a moment, then turned to me with eyebrows raised. I desperately searched my mind for threads, but every one I grasped seemed involved with cheese. From that point on, the conversation took an abstract turn. Details about shipping as a career seemed by general consent to have become irrelevant. And whenever I see a photograph of some Greek shipping magnate on his yacht surrounded by pulchritude, I murmur to myself: 'There, but for an attack of amnesia at Simpson's, go I.'

The outbreak of World War II created a diversion from the pressing problem of my career in life though the elders in my family continued to bear my future in mind.

I entered the lists against Schickelgrüber in October, 1939. As a patriotic rush to arms it was unspectacular—just a matter of popping up to London, being interviewed by the Lieutenant-Colonel of the Grenadier Guards, who assessed my qualities as a leader of men with some probing questions about my prowess with the cricket bat (to which he got some pretty unsatisfactory answers, I can tell you), and going away to await call-up in several months' time. It was the first—and only—time in my life that anyone said to me, 'Don't call us, we'll call you.'

47

By a process not wholly unconnected with nepotism of sorts, I found myself filling in the time, with a cousin of the same age, at a steel works in South Wales—the very same that has since been promoted to *the* Steel Works of South Wales. We were signed on as 'students' at fifteen bob a week, which in those days took care of digs with all found *and* a weekly visit to the movies.

Our landlady in Tan-y-groes Street, Port Talbot, was a mum to us, easing us into our new life on a cushion of almost incessant conversation. She had a lung capacity like blacksmith's bellows and kept up the flow of words until the last cubic millimetre of breath was expended, replenishing the supply with an intake that nearly dragged the tasselled crochet cover off the sideboard. She initiated us at once into the mysteries of high tea. In our hitherto sheltered lives we had known only 'supper' or, on posh occasions, 'dinner'. The first time the mongrel blend of afternoon tea and supper appeared on the table at half past six, I spread strawberry jam all over the cold meats, taking it to be chutney.

It was a rackety life at Tan-y-groes Street. The landlady's husband was bedridden upstairs with the after-effects of a stroke, one of which was that he snored incessantly and, what was worse, irregularly day and night. You never knew when the next burst was coming.

There was another lodger, a Mrs. Mullens, in whom our arrival triggered off acute paranoia. She wore what, as children, we used to call 'dribbling glasses'—gold-rimmed pince-nez secured to her corsage by a thin chain which wobbled like saliva when she bristled indignantly, which she did whenever she clapped eyes on us. Within a week she became convinced that we had engineered a plot to keep her out of the bathroom. If she saw the bathroom door closed, she assumed that one of us was inside, thwarting her hygienic purposes. We would watch her through the chink in our bedroom door, stalking like an

G.W.L., master

. . . . and pupil (on H.L.'s trumpe[t]

deciding not to be a cricketer: H.L. at five

'Dad was a skinhead. . . .'

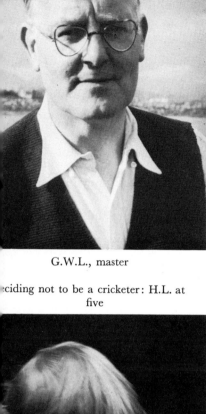

Family discord: Jill, Stephen, Georgina, David, H.L.

The good food scout (*photo David Taylor*)

A touch of the Keir Hardies: Barnet Labour Party march, election '74. Bruce Turner, alto, H.L., trumpet, Georgina Lyttelton, tambourine

Tea and crumpets: H.L. and the Duke

First band. . . .

Present band (1975): l. to r., back row: Tony Mann, Dave Green, Mick Pyne,
front row: Bruce Turner, H.L., Kathy Stobart

enraged hen up and down outside the empty bathroom, her pince-nez dribbling furiously, muttering, 'I know they're in there!' She never actually tried the door-handle, preferring instead to make her presence known by continually pulling the chain of the lavatory next door.

Life as a student in the steel works wasn't initially very exciting. The managers in the various departments were too busy promoting the war effort to give us more than cursory instruction, so we drifted about drawing diagrams in notebooks. I could still give you a rough idea of how a Coke Oven works. As a matter of fact, at any point in the past thirty-five years I could have given you a rough idea of how a Coke Oven works, but no one's ever actually asked. In the circles in which I move now, there aren't many conversational gambits which lead naturally to a rough exposition of the workings of a Coke Oven.

It's just as well, really, because, the first time I saw a Coke Oven in action, it struck me as rather rude. It's an absurdly simple process—coal is fed in at the top and, after a sort of digestive process, coke comes out. It was when I first witnessed the laborious and seemingly rather painful evacuating process that I thought, 'I've heard of art imitating nature, but this is going too far.'

Until I had drawn diagrams of about three hundred pipes and their destinations, I hadn't realised how many by-products come from the coking process. On one occasion, in order to convince us and himself that we were doing something useful, the manager put us on a night-shift in the laboratory where, judging by the pervading smell of naphthalene, they extracted from coal gas the basic ingredient for mothballs. We sat up all night wielding a dip-stick and making crucial tests on the liquid at clearly specified intervals. Or rather, we would have done had we not rather carelessly dropped off at around midnight, waking up in the first light of dawn to the realisation that several critical points in the process had come and gone unrecorded, with heaven knows what consequences.

We hadn't been equipped for life at an expensive public school for nothing, so we dug out the records for the previous week and fudged a convincing-looking entry from them. If you happen to recall a purchase of mothballs, round about Christmas, 1940, which stripped the paper off the bedroom walls, burnt a twelve-inch hole in the back of Dad's Sunday suit and anaesthetised the family cat, I'd be rather obliged if you would keep it quiet.

I won't dwell on the Blast Furnaces, since the transformation of iron ore into molten metal involves those same digestive processes about which we have all heard quite enough already. (It will not surprise you by now that someone whose mind, confronted by the great seething and steaming monuments to man's ingenuity, went straight to human plumbing, failed to make any great headway in industry.) Anyway, it took a long and notably friendless time for it to become known to us that, to the workers, the two strangers haunting the manager's office and snooping about writing in notebooks were clearly spies for the management. We were not helped by the very new-looking cloth caps and dungarees supplied to us by Mr. Lewis in the High Street who, I hardly dare say it, would persist in referring to the latter as 'dungs'. Even after we had surreptitiously sprawled about in coal dust to take the newness out of them, we still felt conspicuous outsiders.

Our status changed when we graduated to the Melting Shop. Here we were discovered by Fred Hurley, a Londoner who, at work, was the charge-hand of the labourers' gang, and in his spare time was the local secretary of Toc H and what was then the British Empire Leprosy Relief Association. He found out somehow that we were distantly related to Gilbert Talbot, in whose memory Toc H had been founded. From that point on he befriended us with such dynamic ruthlessness that we were soon engulfed in altruistic activity—canvassing door-to-door in an Ask-A-Soldier-To-Tea campaign, writing home to Eton to rustle up second-hand books for our lads at sea, even soliciting second-hand pipes from former schoolmasters to send to leper colonies in Africa. Anyone who has ever witnessed the many functions of a schoolmaster's pipe—an instrument for chewing ferociously, waggling facetiously, prodding sagely, puffing ruminatively—will guess that this turned out to be a gruesome collection, but we were assured that they worked wonders in pacifying the patients.

As a counterbalance to these seemingly pious activities, Fred, who had a well-worked and notably unpious repertoire of expletives, introduced us to the beer-drinking marathons at the Velindre Working Men's Club. I have the fondest memories of our Saturday night circle at the V.W.M.C.

Harry, Fred's father-in-law, was one of the Club's elders, a handsome old brigand, tall and straight with a white Clark Gable moustache and a devilishly wild eye in which Fred had learnt to gauge the exact moment in a heavy evening when Harry's mood changed from ripely good-humoured to 'cankerous'. There was old Tom, the perfect foil for the stentorian Harry—round, purple, wheezy and inaudible, with a laugh like a prolonged sneeze. And there was Len, one of your saturnine Welshmen, whose limbs after a pint or two began to wave about, all angular indecision, like those of a puppet. Like all Welshmen, Len was prone to burst into song at the drop of a drop. Unlike most Welshmen, he was quite incapable of singing two consecutive notes in tune. When at the appointed hour he raised his puppet's arms aloft to conduct and launched into his favourite song—a tune of the moment called 'Don't Pass Me By'—Harry would be precipitated into his cankerous phase prematurely. 'Sing a toon, mun, sing a toon!' he would cry, eyes blazing with offended propriety. And old Tom would go blue and start sneezing.

As for the Club itself at that time, I can only recall a bare sort of place in which one sat at wooden tables while pints of wallop, headless, dark brown and lethal, multiplied in front of one as if by trick photography. On most Saturday nights, if the assembled company was in the mood, there would be a 'free and easy'. A chairman for the night would be appointed and would call on those known to have a talent in some form of entertainment to give a turn. There was strict tribal etiquette on these occasions. Ostracism or a heavy toll in free drinks awaited anyone who declined to answer the call when it came. As for the chairman of the night, his standing in the community if not his very manhood depended upon the way he maintained control.

One night, only a short while after we had been introduced into the Club, a 'free and easy' materialised. A man in a flat cap, toothbrush moustache bristling in a promisingly authoritarian fashion, put himself forward as chairman and, having been duly acclaimed, began calling on the entertainers. A young man with no teeth and a cavernous mouth sang 'I mutht go down to the thea again, the lonely thea and the thky . . .' while the front row dodged and weaved and wished themselves in oilskins and sou' westers. Singers predominated, although someone did play 'All through the night' on a musical saw.

When it came to old Tom's turn, the mountain had to come to Mahommed, for his speciality was, like the rest of his personality, inaudible. Against occasions such as this he kept a small tin spoon in his breast pocket with his reading glasses. He remained stolidly in his chair and, as every head in the room bent towards him in wrapt attention, he put the rounded back of the spoon against his teeth and strummed with his fingers on the handle to produce a mouse-like jig.

To Fred, partially deaf since the first war, all the fluttering activity beneath Tom's puce pin-cushion of a nose produced no sound whatsoever, and he began to giggle noisily. When he got up and left the group, I thought it was to compose himself outside. He was in fact making use of the diversion to have a private word with the chairman, with what can only be called malicious intent. Heaven knows what garbled version of my biography he fed into the man's ear or in what scrambled form it finally penetrated his brain. I only know that, when Tom's miniature recital was over, the man in the flat cap banged the table with the flat of his hand and cried 'I now call upon a Member of Parliament, Lord Humpry Lyttelton!'

I should say here that I had no musical instrument with me in Port Talbot at that time, nor was I known to any of my immediate associates there as a musician. Fred's putting forward of my name to the chairman had been conceived and carried out as a joke. In a moment of desperation, I remembered suddenly a sideline with which I had had a modest success at school.

Basically it can be described as animal imitations, with a few film stars thrown in. Partly for dramatic effect and partly to satisfy an overwhelming urge at that moment to shriek, I started with my parrot, following it up for contrast with my goldfish. Seeing old Tom apparently in the throes of hay-fever in the corner, I was encouraged to romp through the whole repertoire—tortoise, cassowary, stork and finally chimpanzee, at which point, overcome by a sort of stagestruck hysteria, I ran amok through the room and took a flying leap on to old Tom's lap.

Modesty prompts me to mince words, but it can be put in no other way. I stopped the show. Indeed, so much beer was needed to revive the gasping audience that the evening fell apart with astonishing speed. Fred's attempt to try the same trick on my cousin failed for the simple reason that the chairman's computer had by now broken down completely beneath the flat cap. Fed with the name 'Mr. Anthony Lyttelton' it hiccupped, blinked, swallowed convulsively, shut its eyes in prolonged concentration and uttered the words 'I now call upon Mr. Rock!!!' Several people began to sing at once in different parts of the room. 'Sing a toon!' bellowed Harry, by now cankerous beyond

53

the reach of all reason. Len, on his way back from his fifteenth expedition to the Gents, took this as his cue and, waving his spidery arms aloft, delivered himself of the words 'Don't pass me by . . .' in the declamatory style later made famous by Rex Harrison, before falling sideways over a table loaded with glasses.

By now the chairman, staring failure in the face, was clinging to Harry's waistcoat and crying like a baby, and Fred, rather overawed by the holocaust that he had unleashed, suggested we should all go home. Our troubles were not quite over. Once outside, Len weaved across to the nearest shadowy lamppost and began to relieve himself against it, singing loud enough to waken the dead. Half way through the operation, the lamppost switched on a torch and arrested him.

Fred Hurley, his wife May, their children and her parents all became our family while we were in Wales. We used to go round to the Hurleys on Sundays—May would serve a vast lunch, after which Fred would take us round to visit his friends. At each house they would express their hospitality with apple or bilberry pies. We would look at Fred in desperation, Fred would seize an opportunity to whisper hoarsely that they would be very offended if we didn't eat a slice or two. By six o'clock it had invariably reached a point of stark choice between eating or breathing. Happily there was a time-limit to this forced-feeding. We had to get back to May—and supper.

As he got to know us, Fred rapidly formed the opinion that it was no bloody good our wandering about the bloody works bloody scribbling in notebooks. The gang of which he was in charge shovelled and humped the ingredients which went into the steel-making furnaces—they had names like dolomite and manganese, but they all looked like grey gravel to us. Under his quite unauthorised guidance we put away our notebooks and set to with shovels. Of all the processes, the Melting Shop, where pig-iron and scrap, seasoned with dolomite and manganese, was brewed into steel, held the most fascination for me.

54

Experts called sample-passers (Oh Lord, here we go again!) could peer into a briefly-opened furnace through hand-held windows of blue glass and tell from the hue of the bubbling mass inside if it was cooking to specification. An élite team of furnacemen, with towels round their necks and little blue spectacles to protect their eyes, 'fettled' the furnace expertly, shovelling up grey gravel and hurling it through the small oven door in one rhythmic movement. They let us fettle a furnace once or twice, demonstrating the technique of which the late Duke Ellington, in another sphere, knew the secret—'It don't mean a thing if it ain't got that swing'. The crane-drivers who lifted the doors only kept them open for a short time, to conserve heat. Interrupt the rhythm, mess up the footwork, and you sent a stream of gravel splatting against the closed door. The first time I tried I forgot to keep a straight shovel and practically decimated the work-force with flying buck-shot.

Our days as outsiders were over. At break-times, we could sit around with the others in the glow of the furnaces, arguing about Churchill, spreading careless talk about where the bombs fell last night and listening to the shop-floor philosopher holding forth. Old William Evans, who looked like Rudyard Kipling, was semi-retired and on light work, so he had plenty of time to wander about refereeing arguments. He had clearly put in a vast amount of reading in his time and had absorbed the gist, if not the actual pronunciation, of a great deal of Western philosophy. If a discussion became too heated, he would douse it by holding up a finger and saying 'As so-and-so said in his great book, *State, Ecclesiasastical and Whaddyercall . . .*'

If my life can be said to have had a single turning-point, the short time in South Wales was it. I came out of it deeply imbued with romantic socialism—a rush of Keir Hardies to the head which I have never lost. There were warm friendships, too, cemented over dominoes at the Velindre Club while up to fifteen pints of beer on a good night gurgled merrily on their way.

Turning About

I HAVE NEVER BEEN one to hark back wistfully to my army days. It's just as well, because the times are hardly propitious for military nostalgia. I keep an old scrap book which contains a few pictures of me in uniform. There's a certain gruesome fascination in the image of myself as a recruit at the Guards Depot at Caterham, cropped like a convict, wearing braces over my shirtsleeve order and sporting size thirteen boots which gleam like molten tar. When I found my children looking at the book a little while ago, I hardly expected cries of patriotic fervour. But I still think that 'Oooo, look! Dad was a skinhead!' went too far in the other direction.

The word 'brainwashing' hadn't been coined when I was at Caterham, but, in practice, the whole system of training there was founded on it. Nowadays, long since rehabilitated or, as the Americans have it, debriefed, I find the state of my footwear so low on my list of priorities that it often gets overlooked for years on end. At a dance once in Thornton Cleveleys (the place is immaterial but a name like that deserves a mention), someone standing close to the stage was overheard to say to his neighbour, 'You can see Humph was in the Guards—look at the shine on those shoes!' He wasn't quite close enough to spot that they were patent leather shoes which I had bought to try and smarten up my lower extremities. Even those didn't last long. We did an open-air show in Barnstaple a few weeks later and they got soaked. Back in the hotel I put them in front of an electric fire to dry off, and they literally curled up and died.

In the light of all this, it's hard even for me to believe now that after about three weeks at Caterham, I was a fanatic about my toe-caps. The treatment which we meted out to those poor boots hardly bears description. It involved 'boning' them with the handle of a toothbrush to iron out the pores of the leather, smearing them with boot-polish and setting fire to it to harden the surface and—a real old soldier's dodge, this one—peeing in them and leaving them overnight to marinate, as it were, until the leather became brittle and receptive to the polish. After the war had been going on for a year or two, some perceptive fellow at the War Office noticed that the requisition for new boots from the Brigade of Guards exceeded those of the rest of the British army put together. It took no more than a brief test on one ammoniated boot to find out why, so the order went out that boots were to be shiny no longer. But not before I had discovered that three weeks was all it need to mould me into a mindless zombie who thought nothing of piddling in his boots.

Looking back, it strikes me that most of the people one encountered in the army were stark, staring mad. Sometimes, supervising a parade as an officer and watching drill-sergeants and sergeant-majors going through extraordinary paroxysms and facial contortions, it occurred to me that, in civilian life, people were shut away for much less. It was clear that the maintenance of discipline required a total suspension of a sense of humour. When I was stationed as a lieutenant at Wellington Barracks—the place from which the troops emerge for the world-famous Changing of the Guard—a quite serious crisis of discipline occurred over an incident which, to most of us part-timers, seemed trivial and mildly hilarious.

It was discovered, at crack of dawn, that someone had, in the

euphemistic language of Army Regulations, committed a nuisance in the middle of the parade ground. No one knew when it had happened but, when daylight broke and soldiers began to turn out for the early parade, there it was, quite substantial and for all to see. Hasty work with a shovel would, one might think, have been the simplest way of, well, clearing up the matter. But before this could be done, the Regimental Sergeant-Major had come on to the scene and had been, to put it mildly, appalled. To him, the offending object in the parade-ground was not simply a nuisance—it was a symbol of defiance, an act of mutiny, a studied and deliberate insult to Her Majesty's tarmac.

Before the sun had risen above the cookhouse block, a culprit had been pursuaded to confess and was duly marched in front of the commanding-officer. He gave the only possible explanation in the circumstances—that, having drunk some beer in a pub which had upset his digestion, he had been taken short halfway across the parade-ground with an attack of the 'runs'. The R.S.M. would have none of this. 'I thank you, sir, for leave to speak!' he bellowed in the lunatic formula required. 'Sir, I personally hexamined the nuisance with my pace-stick and found it hard and hobviously made with a heffort!'

I never made the most of officer's mess life, largely because if ever I was within reach of London I used to go off on my own listening to jazz and, as time went on, playing it. Besides, social workers have a word for me, and it's 'unclubbable'. It was coined to designate those who hang about loutishly on street corners instead of joining youth clubs or darts teams as nature intended, and I am prepared to accept that they didn't have me specifically in mind. But the cap fits, and I wear it with a certain amount of jaunty defiance. Some people were born to join things, others were not. When I am approached by some eager lady with the words 'Mr Lyttelton, I'm going to rope you in . . . .' (and we unclubbables can spot one of nature's cowboys a mile off) I don't hang about to hear for what purpose I am to be rounded up. With eyes rolling and nostrils steaming, I'm off across the plains at a brisk gallop, whinnying my excuses.

There is no limit to the opportunities for social advancement that I have passed up through innate unclubbability. As a young Guards Officer at large in London after the war, with so many eligible young men still posted overseas, I was strongly in the running as a Deb's Delight. Instead of which, whenever Ball Committees met and invitation lists were drawn up, the order went forth, 'Don't ask that young man with the big feet who stands by the band all night long!'

There were Royal occasions, too, when a finger seemed to beckon me through half-open doors towards that most exclusive of clubs which surrounded the young princesses. I still have, in a drawerful of oddments, an invitation by Royal Command to 'a small informal dance at Windsor Castle on Thursday, 25th March, 1943'. Not one of your great faceless, impersonal State Balls, mark you, but an informal dance, and a small one at that. Just George, Elizabeth, Lillibet, Margaret and me, with perhaps a couple of hundred odds and sods thrown in to make up the numbers.

Before going into the ballroom, we were briefed by a court official on such details as how to bow to the Royal Family on presentation, not bending from the waist in an ostentatious fashion but letting the head loll forward as though the neck muscles had momentarily given way. Since I was six foot three and Princess Margaret was three foot six, the exercise was rather more complicated than the court official made out, but by bending the knees surreptitiously, I think I carried it off all right. It was the band that let me down. It was Geraldo's Orchestra, at that time liberally peppered with names held in awe by youthful readers of the *Melody Maker* and *Rhythm*. The late Ted Heath was on trombone, Nat Temple sat in the saxophone section and the star trumpet soloist was Leslie 'Jiver'

Hutchinson, a particular idol of mine.

Well, nobody actually said anything to me about standing glued to the bandstand all night, but you don't become King without getting to know at a glance the difference between a clubman and a loiterer on street corners, and you may have noticed on your telly that I wasn't at the Royal Wedding a year or two ago. In fact, the whole dance ended on a rather unpropitious note. Some of the copious supply of champagne found its way down below to the guardroom where some guardsmen in my company were on duty as firewatchers. Leaving their inhibitions below stairs among the firebuckets and stirrup-pumps, they surfaced in a state of some disarray to watch the guests departing. Two of them went so far as to line up unsteadily alongside the Royal party, presenting arms with their incendiary-bomb shovels and grinning inanely.

Out of six years in the army I spent one month actually fighting to save civilisation as we know it, which seems rather a waste of this particular unit of manpower. My army career ended on a surrealistic note. In 1946, some lunatic at the War Office decided that the time was ripe for a nationwide recruiting drive. They put together what they called a Mobile Demonstration Column which was, in effect, a sort of military circus. We lumbered off round the country like Billy Smart's in khaki, setting up in fields and on football grounds where the PT boys did gymnastics, the military police performed on motorbikes, the artillery and the tank chaps let kids swarm all over their guns and tanks, and the dental corps, by way of a side show, demonstrated how they made military false teeth. Though I say it myself (and as adjutant to the whole show I was responsible for the fact that, four out of five times, we hit the right town at the right time) it was rather impressive.

It was said when we got back that we had attracted one recruit but that three of our chaps had deserted. I think it was only a rumour.

62

Nosh & Gigs

Eating Around

ONE OF SEVERAL REASONS why I am not a millionaire today is that, when I was demobbed in 1946, I neglected to invest my gratuity in some burgeoning enterprise. Instead, I spent it, all £88 of it, on Chinese food. One evening after a recording session, John Dankworth introduced me to the now defunct Universal Chinese Restaurant in Denmark Street and I was instantly hooked.

The symptoms were like those of any other addiction. I became shifty and unreliable. I devised brutishly cunning deceptions to skip classes at the Camberwell Art School, signing the register at the door in the morning and then doubling back out on all fours so as to catch a bus into town and achieve my midday fix of pancake roll and fried spring cabbage. That same evening I would be back again, cramming in soft noodles, meat balls and stewed green pea without pausing to wonder how you stew a green pea.

I was in my middle twenties then, presumably at the tail-end of that highly sensitised period in life when things taste and smell as they will never taste and smell again. Certainly I have pursued, like the Holy Grail, the ecstasy of those first Chinese meals. But with the taste buds worn flat and shiny like the hobnails in a favourite pair of boots, it is gone almost beyond recollection. Perhaps those meals impressed so vividly because they were oases in a barren desert of student feeding. At Camberwell we used to eat in a café round the corner, drinking rust-remover tea out of thick china cups and watching the proprietor pressing slabs of cheese into spherical bread rolls with a finger that was permanently encased in an ageing, blackening bandage. We used to ask for cheese-and-ptomaine rolls.

Within a year or so of those art-student days I was eating my way around the country first with George Webb's Dixielanders and then with my own band. On the face of it, touring musicians, like commercial travellers, are unsound consultants when it comes to food. They spend a large part of their lives exploring the very depths of British culinary practice. In otherwise civilised towns, they have stayed at hotels in which dinner *ends* at seven-thirty and where, thenceforward, the only choice is between seedy snack-bars or a Chinese restaurant in which to order 'Sweet and Sour' is to embark on a dispiriting game of Hunt the Pork.

They know what it is to choose between night-starvation and a transport 'caff' where the troughs in the charred bacon hold enough grease' to maintain a heavy lorry from Penzance to Perth. In the course of duty they have eaten alleged food which seems to have been hand-knitted, carved out of balsa wood, barbecued by blow-lamp or assembled in a laboratory. For this reason, they are perhaps too easily pleased. Set before them a dish of scrambled eggs which does not suggest, by taste and texture, that it has been finished off in a spin-drier, and they will go into raptures.

After years of taking pot-luck in this way, I was considerably startled when Hugh Johnson, once described rather surrealistically as 'one of the world's great palates' and then editor of *Queen Magazine*, wrote asking me to contribute their restaurant reviews page. It began as a 'guest' article for one issue only, and like the aunt who comes for a week-end and stays a lifetime, I've been doing it ever since. To be frank, I've never really seen myself as a food-writer for a glossy mag. I think of them as trendy, fashionable people with a zest for night life. I am no Night Person. My preordained bedtime is midnight, and at the stroke of twelve I turn into a pumpkin. Even as a young man, the cry of 'Let's go on somewhere!' would send me scurrying into the nearest Gents to lurk behind locked doors until they had all gone. My reluctance to believe in life after death may well stem from some subconscious disinclination to 'go on somewhere' when I could be tucked up snugly in my eternal bed.

As for trendiness, I am a firm believer in the theory that, for someone of irregular shape for whom buying clothes is a chore rather than a hobby, the best way to be in fashion at least some of the time is to stand perfectly still and let trends come round to you.

Mind you, I have had my moments. It is not generally known that, in the very vanguard of fashion, I once had an Edwardian suit made, with narrow trousers, pinched waist and flared jacket. I had been wearing it for some months when it received the official seal of approval. I was playing at a concert at the Regal cinema, Edmonton, and in a nearby pub during the interval, my wife overheard the following conversation between two Teddy Boys in full regalia.

'That 'Umphrey Lyttelton. . . .'

'What abaht 'im?'

''E's one of us!'

It must be admitted that the suit was not an unmitigated success. For some reason best known to the Edwardians, the trousers came right up under my armpits, held up by the shortest pair of braces outside of a circus. There came a time, after a certain amount of fashionable eating-out appropriate to my new status as a trend-setter, when I began to experience a sort of creeping asphyxia. So I gave the suit away to the WVS and

reverted to my pristine bagginess. To this day, I sometimes have twinges of conscience at the thought of some old-age pensioner or earthquake victim incarcerated in those trousers, thrashing about in the dark and calling for help.

Leaving aside these private feelings of incongruity, I have enjoyed being a food scout for *Harpers & Queen*. Of course, there comes a time in every man's life, if he is not encased like a rhinoceros in three inches of armour plating, when he stops dead in his tracks and asks! 'What am I doing here? What's it all about, Alfie?'

The food scout is particularly prone to this sort of self-interrogation. For one thing his job doesn't, to the casual observer, look very much like work. Slaving away over a hot carré d'agneau Arlésienne isn't the kind of hard labour that attracts sympathy or even admiration. Union chiefs will not lose sleep over his man hours nor call a strike if a recalcitrant waiter or a brandy or two in the course of duty run him into overtime.

What is even more disconcerting is the conviction that washes over him with almost tidal regularity that he is performing no useful function. What, when all is said and done, does he actually *do?* When a new restaurant opens he goes trotting off quite prepared, in that selfless way which stamps his job as a vocation rather than a mere profession, to expose himself to ptomaine poisoning, botulism, trencherman's elbow, bubonic plague, the gryppe and whatever else is going for the benefit of his fellow men.

On arrival he finds the place teeming with people who have got to hear about it through some more speedy and efficient grapevine than his own. There they all are, golloping up the food without waiting for his judgment, braying deliriously over the divine decor and the madly groovy waiters and calling the proprietor Freddie, 'Luigers' or Bimbi in tones of long familiarity.

If, in the midst of all this conviviality, your food-scout detects that eighty per cent of the food has come from tins and that the wine-waiter is concealing a profound ignorance behind a lot of cork-sniffing and napkin-flapping, then he feels like that horrid little boy at a children's party who heckles the ventriloquist with, 'It's him! I saw his lips move!'

Perhaps one invites these deflationary feelings by taking the job too seriously. It's healthy and indeed essential for a critic of anything to remind himself over and over again that the object of his criticism, be it literature, art, music or food, will continue blithely on its way without a backward glance if he were suddenly to fall under a bus. The only food critic whose views have any relevance is the person who, at any given point in time, is actually eating the food. His opinions would hardly fill a paragraph, let alone a page, being expressed in terms of 'Yum Yum!' or 'Uaaarrrgh!' with various inarticulate shades of doubt and indecision in between. Or look at it another way. When it comes to fish and chips, your genuine pundit is neither the food snob who never touches them on principle, nor the inverted food snob who eats them once in a while with a great show of democratic zeal. No, it's the man who eats them every Friday night, year in year out. He never opens his mouth, except to pop in a chip or a lump of cod. But he knows, yer know.

There is also the ire of disappointed noshers to contend with. Contrary to the belief of all restaurateurs and many readers, food-scouts are kindly folk. We are not hired assassins or hatchet-men. We don't relish, or indeed comply with, the frequently-received exhortations from those who have had a bad meal to go in and take the offending place apart. Sometimes however, our very kindness brings disaster upon a new restaurant which we hoped to encourage.

70

I once went to a place where the food was enterprising and good, but where the service, of the eager debutante type quite common in Knightsbridge, teetered dangerously on the verge of calamity. I thought the restaurant worth encouraging, and wrote about it with some enthusiasm. So did Quentin Crewe in *Vogue*, and our articles came out almost simultaneously. Prompted by our unanimous praise, readers rushed to the place in large numbers—and under the strain, the hard-pressed service collapsed. I had been rather charmed by a waitress who, on bringing up a fiery-looking liquid in a small jug, was asked 'Is that a hot sauce?' and, putting an elegantly manicured hand to the jug, answered 'Well, it's quite warm.' But some of my readers who followed up my recommendation were less enchanted.

It's then that the rude letters pour in. I once concocted a sort of standard letter of complaint—caricatured, but not altogether untypical.

Dear Sir,

Acting solely on your recommendation in *Queen*, my wife and I took two friends to the Lucretia Borgia restaurant a few evenings ago. I think you should be informed of our experience.

You describe the service there as 'attentive, careful and friendly'. I concede that it was attentive of the waiter to draw back my wife's chair as she approached the table. But his omission to replace it under her as she sat down can hardly be called 'careful'. And if the cries of 'Heave ho, me hearties!' and 'Fifteen bob a hundredweight!' from the staff as they helped her from the floor come within your interpretation of 'friendly', then it is the kind of friendliness we can well do without.

I will not dwell overlong on those items euphemistically listed in the (exorbitant and wrongly added-up) bill as FOOD. I asked for my steak rare. It arrived on the table

71

raw—so raw, in fact, that I was bitten quite severely on the thumb, incurring a wound deep enough to require, on the advice of my doctor, precautionary innoculation against tetanus and rabies. My friends, anxious to put your comments to a fair test, decided to sample the crab-apple soufflé which you found 'exquisite'. The joint inquest takes place on Friday.

By ten-thirty, when according to your report the place is 'really swinging', all the table-cloths had been removed and the chairs stacked on the tables, including those on which we were sitting. Needless to say, I did not leave a tip. And in future I shall take your recommendations with a pinch of salt.

Yours in disgust,
Regular Reader

For someone who had always taken a cursory interest in the technicalities of *cuisine* there was a lot to learn. And that takes practical experience as well as a handy gastronomic dictionary. Take Coupe Jacques, for instance—and if you travel the lesser hotels of Britain, you will have to, sooner or later, as an alternative to Various Ices and Cheddar Cheese. In gastronomic guide books, Coupe Jacques is spoken of with respect—indeed, the fact that it is mentioned at all indicates that there must have been a time and a circumstance when this cup of mingled fruits and ice-cream merited consideration as a sweet. But go into the Station Hotel, Upper Spagforth and ask for that same Coupe Jacques and you will get a saccharine concoction of tinned fruit, syrup and frozen plaster amounting to a defamation of character for which Jacques, whoever he may be, should seek reparation in the courts.

There are more subtle shades of meaning to be found in culinary names, as I have found in six years of food exploration. If you go to places where they do French cooking, you will probably find on the menu something called *poulet grand'mère*. In Haute Cuisine, this will mean chicken sauté-ed with a rich brown grand'mère sauce added at the climactic moment of cooking. In Provincial, Regional or Country cooking, on the other hand, the same words will convey chicken cooked in casserole with wine and vegetables and as like as not served by a grand'mère, probably wearing bedroom-slippers. In Basse Cuisine, the title that should go officially to a high percentage of British restaurant food, it will simply mean that the chicken *is* grand'mère.

It's not enough nowadays to learn off all the familiar terms which appear in French on the average 'classic' menu. I'll come to the food of all nations in a minute, but there has also been an upsurge of English nationalism in the culinary field. Up until a few years ago, there were two kinds of restaurant purveying English food. One catered unashamedly for chauvinists, offering great carcases of beef or mutton that has quite clearly not been 'mucked about'. The other went in more for sporty things like pheasant, venison, pigeon-pie and game paté and often laboured the hunting theme in style and decor as if to try and give the diner a vicarious thrill of the chase.

Now there's a third style, and it involves scouring old English cookery-books for ancient recipes that long ago fell into disuse. Staunch isolationists who have long campaigned against menus written in a foreign tongue will find little practical comfort in this new trend. There is not even a handy pocket dictionary available to plumb the mysteries of names like Mrs Trusgrove's Hot Grummet, Skirret and Oatmeal Furdy Pot, Rutlandshire Groatle Cakes or Cobbler's Platter. The fact that I made all those up only goes to show the extent to which the innocent diner-out is at the mercy of ruthless and imaginative food-lorists. A Thomas Hardy-esque name, a handful of oats and a blob of honey and who, without recourse to the British Museum, will be any the wiser?

Despite the noticeable advance in the 'Eat British' movement, most of the stuff we pay to devour is alien rather than indigenous. There are two ways of approaching foreign food. (Actually, there are three, but we'll leave out 'all upset tummies begin at Calais'.)

I can best define them as the dedicated and the pragmatic. The dedicated eater, visiting a national restaurant of whatever denomination, aims to immerse himself in the gastronomic culture of the country concerned. He is the one you will find grappling bravely with chopsticks, wincing over undrinkable local wines and suppressing the instincts of a lifetime in the face of raw fish. His motto is 'When in Rome, eat as the Romans do', and if some convincing joker were to tell him that in some areas of Rome they eat the table mats, then eat them he will, cork, Canaletto reproduction and all.

The pragmatic eater's motto is less high-minded. It is 'Sod the Chinese, if I want chop suey and chips, I'll have 'em!' While not admitting to a craving for that particular dish, it is an attitude with which I have some sympathy. To put it crudely, our colon was not designed for culture nor our taste buds for tourism. There is a story that Bishop Gore, an eminent theologian in the early part of this century, was in America when Grape-nuts first came on to the market as a new breakfast cereal. At breakfast in a hotel, the new product was proudly set before him. He gazed down into the bowl for some moments and then spoke, enunciating each syllable with scathing precision. 'Gravel! I positively refuse to eat gravel!'

For myself, I positively refuse to drink turpentine. Not long ago, I took home a bottle of Greek *retsina*. If you have not yet come across this name and imagine that it has some connection with resin, then you are perfectly right. Having broached the bottle and battled through a glass of the stuff, I left it on the draining board in the kitchen. Next day, feeling strong enough to have another try, I went to find it. Seeing me looking around by the sink, our daily came to my assistance. 'Are you looking for that bottle? I put it in the garage with your other painting things.' And in the garage it stayed.

You can put me down then as a pragmatic eater. If I go to a specialised national restaurant, it is for the same reason that I go to any restaurant—to have a good meal of my own choice, not to endure purgatory and emerge feeling like an issue of the *National Geographical Magazine*.

It's in the field of foreign food that good-foodmanship is most rife. I once had to give up reading magazines altogether because of an acute inferiority complex, acquired through learning week after week about someone or other whose car had broken down in a remote part of Europe and who had been served a classic and incomparable dish in a nearby farmhouse while waiting for the man from the garage. At the time, I had just been on a motoring holiday in France during which my car had broken down in every conceivable circumstance, and all I ever got was a slab of veal, *pommes frites* and salad—very welcome, too, but hardly the thing to bring out with a flourish in a concourse of gourmets.

Happily, I sense that, in these days of the anti-hero and the kitchen-sink, this sort of romantic and retrospective lip-smacking is going out of fashion. It's the man who can boast of having survived absolutely diabolical food who will soon be scoring one-upmanship points. When this time comes, I am ready. Clear in my mind is the memory of a little restaurant in a backstreet in Algiers back in '43, when the genial *patron*, showing broken teeth in a welcoming smile beneath his black, brigand's moustache, set before me a local dish looking like baked tennis socks and tasting indescribably of *je ne sais quoi*. (Actually, *je sais quoi* perfectly well, but *je ne veux pas* mention it in polite company.)

That was during the war. Since then, on sundry tours when playing concerts has been the primary purpose and eating has had to be fitted in when and where possible, I've had plenty of opportunity to investigate the cuisines and customs of other nationalities from unusual angles. My thoughts about Dutch food were coloured irrevocably by an incident in 1948, when I first took my band to play in Amsterdam. In those days, foreign tours were run on a shoe-string, and for economy we were housed in an improvised dormitory at the top of a tall house owned by one of the young promoters. On the first night, after the concert, we underwent a reaction understandable, if not excusable, in a group of red-blooded young English men suddenly released from ration books, licensing laws and spam. In short, we took Amsterdam apart. Dawn was breaking when we clawed our way up the narrow stairs to our communal pad.

Two hours later, our Dutch host, anxious that his accommodation should make up in hospitality what it lacked in the finer comforts, brought us breakfast. Each of us in turn was nudged and prodded into consciousness to be confronted with a large plate around which were arranged several slices of dark, close-textured bread of the pumpernickel variety. On each slice was a different item of food—on one a square of cold beef, on the next a slab of cheese and then, in rotation, apricot jam, gherkin, some kind of pressed meat and finally, and quite incredibly, a wedge of fruit cake.

Linger for a moment on the sensation. The mouth feels like the ornithological equivalent of a Rachman-style basement in Paddington that has just been vacated hurriedly by two parrots of a feckless disposition and untidy habits. In place of the clear, cool and mobile brow of yesterday is now a rusty, creaking visor behind which a large animal suspiciously like an adult porcupine has clearly moved in for the winter. A binding substance made seemingly of axle-grease, brown sugar and ash-tray scrapings prevents the eyelids from parting to admit the unwelcome light of day. When they do finally open enough to let in a shaft of vision, the cringeing gaze alights, with a slow-dawning horror, on a still life of dry bread and fruit cake.

It was, all in all, a mutually educative experience. We learned of the importance of bread in the domestic economy of Holland, while our host was offered a quite unique insight into some of the more expressive and creative aspects of the English language. The matter, alas, did not end there. Later in the day, when with restored spirits we set off in search of steaks and schnitzels, he insisted on being our guide. He took us straight to what looked like a Lyons Corner House and asked with bland innocence: 'What kind of sandwich do you like?' With his limited command of English he was spared from knowing just how close he came at that moment to being pitched into the canal with his feet encased in a ballast of rye bread.

We once played a three-week engagement in Berne, in a rather posh night-club. At the end, the owner came to our dressing room to say a formal goodbye. He made a speech thanking us for coming and regretting that the attendances had not reached his expectations (on most nights it would have needed a tyre-lever to prise an extra person into the place). His peroration was rather moving. 'In Switzerland we are famous for our watches and our cheese. Because business has been not so good, I cannot thank you with watches, so . . .' and he went over to a cupboard and flung open the door, revealing a stack of cheeses the size of mini-car wheels, '. . . I thank you with cheese!'

To the Swiss, cheese is a national symbol. It represents industry, thrift, self-reliance, all the things of which they are most proud. They will not only thank you with cheese, they will entice, impress, reprove and even threaten you with cheese. I know of several national dishes—especially those involving chillies or cayenne pepper—which can assume to the unwary all the characteristics of a rather nasty practical joke. But surely the Swiss cheese *fondue* is alone in actually posing a threat to life. I hardly dare touch the stuff myself, having been warned on so many occasions that a swig of the wrong sort of drink will solidify the molten cheese into a cannonball somewhere in my alimentary canal, sending me plummeting to the ground and probably through the floor boards.

Some years ago at the end of a Swiss tour, Joe Temperley, who was then playing baritone sax in the band, rounded off an afternoon of festive sightseeing by sitting down to a *fondue* backed up by several large glasses of chilled beer. He caused consternation in the restaurant. Every time he lifted the beer glass to his lips, people waved their arms and cried 'No, No!' as if he were a prospective suicide poised on a ledge. One total stranger, signalling frantically, sent over to his table a glass of the medically approved *kirsch*. My friend downed it with a genial cry of 'Cheers!' and took another mighty swig of beer as a chaser.

Joe didn't actually plummet. Indeed, when he met us for the journey home, he was already so near the ground that there was no margin left for plummeting. His face had assumed the most extraordinary hue that can only be compared to the northward view of a south-bound baboon, and he had such difficulty with his breathing that we were almost persuaded to send for a man with a stomach-pump. In the event, high altitude seemed to do him good and he recovered slowly during the flight, but was still so mottled and crimson on arrival in London that a fellow-musician suggested he go home with him for an hour or two to regain a more natural colour before he confronted his wife. It was just his bad luck that the fellow-musician's Swedish wife, forewarned of a guest, hurriedly prepared a welcoming meal consisting almost entirely of cheese.

Maybe I have undervalued the role of the travelling minstrel in the service of gastronomy. Certainly we have lacked neither enterprise nor courage. There's a favourite musicians' haunt in

Dusseldorf—or was when I last went there—called *Czikos,* which specialises in Hungarian food. It's all wooden planks, rope banisters and gypsy violins, and it serves a shashlik on wooden plates for which people come for miles. Into this, like the joke spider in a Christmas stocking, is inserted the odd green chilli, looking as innocent as a runner bean but capable of blowing the roof off your head. The chief speciality, however, is a goulash soup so hot that it is issued, not as a food at all, but as a naked challenge. Two American soldiers dined there one night, and after the meal, when they were collecting their coats from the cloakroom, they asked to see the proprietor. When he appeared, one of them floored him with a blow, saying, 'That's for the soup, buddy!'

Much valuable exploratory work in the field of Indo-Pakistani restaurants has been done in the past by touring musicians caught up in a backlash against insipid hotel meals and hamburger bars with standing room only. In every large industrial town they sought out, by trial and error, at least one *Taj Mahal, Koh-I-Noor* or *Star of Asia* where, despite crumbling decor, the food is excellent.

I was, literally, in the front line at the height of this movement. Part of my band's stage show was a version by vocal trio of 'The Whiffenpoof Song,' in which my two saxophone players and I would converge on the front microphone to sing: 'We are poor little lambs who have lost our way, baa...baa...baa!' Joe Temperley and Tony Coe were both in the throes of acute Madras Curry addiction at the time and, huddled together as we were in close harmony, the first 'baa' used to hit me like a sirocco. We always gave each 'baa' the full value of a dotted minim, and the second one was timed to catch me just as I came up for air. By the third, it was clear to those in the remotest corner of the auditorium that the lead singer was suffering some kind of paroxysm and that only his arms draped in a clubman's embrace around his colleagues' shoulders were preventing him

The Whiffenpoof Song—
curried style

from slumping to the floor. I soon discovered that the only way to meet this problem was to get to an Indian restaurant first and work up a counterblast. In this way I gained sufficient experience, if not to tell other people what they should like, at least to know what I like.

On the other hand I have never really got to grips with vegetarian food. Vegetarianism is rife among musicians, and I have been through all the familiar arguments. Freddy Grant, a West Indian colleague, with whom I toured once, used to insist that if God had meant us to eat meat, he would have given us sharp teeth. He treated my argument that God gave us steak knives instead, with less consideration than it deserved. The final rift came when he pressed me to eat a sort of wholewheat rock-cake which he had made himself and which was as solid and unpenetrable as oak. 'If God had meant me to eat that,' I said, 'he would have given me teeth like a hacksaw.'

I shall be mentioning American visitors to this country later in the book, but this seems an appropriate place to pay tribute to some of the most formidable eaters I ever encountered. I had always regarded myself as a pretty fair trencherman until the day in 1958—in Leeds, of all places—when I witnessed a gastronomic duel between two visiting Americans. One was Bobby—valet, hairdresser and general factotum to Duke Ellington, as bald and bulky as a Japanese wrestler. The other, 'Little' Jimmy Rushing, blues-singer extraordinary and the original Mister Five by Five—tipping, not to say demolishing, the scales at twenty-odd stone. Ordering the meal was an auction, each one outbidding the other in the number of pork chops and fried eggs he proposed to eat. I suspect that the outcome was a draw, though I have no clear memory. My mind was too busy boggling at the statistics—sixteen pork chops, ten fried eggs, several hundredweight of chips, two office blocks of apple pie and enough coffee to float them home across the Atlantic with a full Royal Navy escort and all flags flying.

81

Jimmy Rushing always insisted that his size had nothing to do with over-eating ('I was born fat,' he told us), and it's true that on tour he often kept going on the lightest of snacks for days on end. But from the few occasions when we saw him perform in championship style, it was clear that some heavy training was going on in secret. I took him to an Italian restaurant once after a session at my club in Oxford Street. He was in the mood for some serious eating and asked me to order him the 'best steak in the house'. Misjudging his taste I ordered him a prime filet which so depleted my budget for the evening that I had to go myself for the cheapest thing on the menu. This was a plain escalope of veal, which arrived hammered so flat that it overlapped the edges of the plate. Jim looked at his steak, which was ten times thicker but covered a much smaller area of the plate. With a rueful expression he looked back at my great floppy sheet of escalope. As the host I felt it incumbent upon me to alleviate his obvious disappointment, so we swapped plates with mutual satisfaction.

I had forgotten the importance of size in any American assessment of a good steak. From then on I had plenty of reminders. When I drove Marie Knight, a handsome and formidable gospel-singer, around Britain some years ago on a tour, she clearly regarded our food as positively sinful.

In desperation I took her to the Leofric Hotel in Coventry, where the French restaurant was something of an oasis in the Midlands. I ordered her the best steak in the house, and when it arrived, she called for meat sauce—the bottled kind which will restore a blackened penny to mint condition in ten seconds flat—and obliterated the steak from view. Seeing my lower lip trembling, she explained that *small steaks have no taste*.

One of the most prodigious eaters I ever met is blues-singer Big (six foot and twenty-four stone, as a matter of fact) Joe Turner. When he toured with me, we stopped one morning in North London, on the way home, so that he could buy himself a

Jimmy Rushing contemplates an English steak.

steak for lunch. The butcher brought out a long strip of rump and, hovering over it with a knife, asked how big a steak he wanted. 'I'll take it all,' was the reply, and this huge mattress of meat was rolled up and put in a bag. The story has an appalling sequel. Getting back to his apartment, he lit the electric stove and put the steak (folded three ways, no doubt) under the grill. He then lay on the bed and went to sleep for two hours, with results on which we need not dwell.

Gigging Around

AS I HAVE SAID BEFORE, in the context of food, the touring musician is as likely to become a connoisseur of the bad things of life as of the good. Like actors in the days of Henry VIII, dance-band musicians—and jazzmen are inextricably mixed in with them—are generally regarded by their fellow men today as rogues and vagabonds. We don't simply incur bad experiences, we positively invite them. Some incidents, mind you, attain a sort of classic virtue by their very badness. I cherish the exchange I had with a choleric old man when, in a car loaded with instruments, I stopped on the outskirts of Bradford to ask him the way to the University. 'What university?' he shouted back impatiently. 'Bradford University,' I said. 'There isn't one!' he cried, making as if to walk on. 'There must be!' I called after him, 'I'm playing there tonight.' In a paroxysm of rage, he turned round. 'WELL, WHERE IS IT THEN?'

We suffer particularly from the staff in small hotels who seem, as often as not, to exult in finding, in these sluggards who lie a-bed all morning and keep demanding food and drink at all hours, orders lower than themselves. Usually, the sadistic refusal of night-porters to cooperate in providing refreshment late at night simply makes for ugliness and bad feeling. But there was something faintly endearing about the snowy-haired retainer at a hotel in North Wales who insisted, in accents of deep regret, that he could not lay his hands on so much as a bottle of light ale. It was only midnight so we pressed our rights as bona fide travellers. 'There's nothing I can do, sir!' he said. 'The manager has the key to the drink cupboard and he has gone to bed.' 'Then wake him up!' we cried to a man. The old boy started back in horror. 'Don't ask me to do that, sir,' he begged. 'The manager's had a hard life!'

Chambermaids, too, succumb to latent sadism whenever they suspect that one would like to sleep into the morning after working late. They have a set routine, probably laid out in the training manual, for flushing late-risers out from between the sheets. It begins with persistent knocking until the victim shows himself by muffled protests to be awake. Then a bunch of keys are brought into action, to be rattled meaningfully in the lock, accompanied by mutinous muttering. Some minutes later the uneasy doze which has now replaced sleep will be shattered by an earsplitting burst from the bed-side telephone. It is the receptionist who has now been brought in as reinforcement. 'Did you ask for a call, sir?' she asks ingenuously. I once had a tenacious lady follow up my anguished denial with another call to say, 'It's all right, sir—it wasn't your call, it was for No. 9!'

If it's any comfort you can usually win if you hold out long enough. The barrage of Hoovers which opens up at mid-morning may sound frightening but can do no harm if you stay put. Appeals to your better nature are hardest to resist. A chambermaid in Staffordshire once got me to surrender, when all else had failed, by calling through the locked door, 'Come on, love, be a sport—let's 'ave yer sheets!'

There's a general belief that all this hardship is offset by the glamorous, not to say erotic, situations into which the dance-band musician is thrown by nature of his work. And here I must admit failure. Other musicians seem ready, at the drop of a paper hat, to recall festive occasions at which, by the end of the first cha-cha, the dance-floor has become an uncensored dramatisation of the correspondence columns of *Penthouse* magazine. I always get the other kind.

There was, it is true, this society ball in Surrey some years ago, at which fairground swings and nightwatchman's brasiers had been set up in the grounds as a diversion. Rumour reached the bandstand via our car driver—a notoriously unreliable source whose career in the car-hire business seemed to be spent exclusively in driving high-ranking public figures to clandestine and kinky assignations—that from the highest point of the swings, unmentionable scenes could be observed taking place in the roseate glow of distant fires. I am always slow off the mark on these occasions and never even made the queue. But circumstantial evidence did support his story, since for the rest of the night the swings were monopolised by men, all heaving away at the ropes like bellringers of Hades.

I have to report that the Playboy culture, with its bacchanalian office-parties and carefree partner-swapping, is still several million light-years away from the average firm's dance in Chelmsford or Stoke-on-Trent. Sexologists may be able to read some deep erotic significance into the Hokey Cokey. From my viewpoint on the bandstand, all that putting your left leg in, your left leg out, your left leg in and shaking it all about resembles nothing more than one of those sublimating activities, like cricket, which public schools invent to keep the boys from base and debilitating habits.

My trouble with the Hokey Cokey is that I never know when to stop. When I'm in charge of the music the revellers soon run out of arms and legs and are compelled, as verse succeeds verse interminably, to put in, put out and shake about quite unaccustomed parts of their anatomy. But even with this encouragement nothing very exciting ever happens.

At first sight there seems more of a hint of Eastern promise in the Conga. For one thing, its movements—three slithery, hip-wiggling steps and then a coy sideways kick like an indolent dog cocking its leg—have a certain sensuousness. But whatever hot-blooded and abandoned Latin-American ways were imported with the dance, you can rest assured that the traditional puritanism of the English ballroom long since put paid to them. While not quite so crudely sadistic as the Paul Jones, which was surely designed by some committee of Mrs. Grundys to nip burgeoning relationships in the bud, the Conga, English-style, has enough built-in precautions to frustrate any hanky-panky. If, despite the counter-aphrodisiac properties of bottled beer and cold sausage rolls, a participant should become so inflamed by the sight of the undulating hips in front of him as to try and steer their owner off in the direction of the bedrooms, there in tow behind him are two hundred perspiring chaperones, one-and-two-and-three-hopping along in pursuit and checking his ardour with passion-deadening slogans like 'Ay ay, Fred's at it again!' 'Put it down, you don't know where it's been!' and ''Ow's the wife?' It's little wonder that, like some great thwarted serpent, the Conga-line so often turns violent and heads for the bandstand, vengefully knocking over the music and treading on the instruments.

If the music at the traditional English 'hop' is often indescribably bad, it's unfair to put all the blame on the musicians. I'd just like to see Johann Strauss having to cope with a Spot Dance, for instance, and being called upon to arrest the 'Blue Danube' in full flood whenever some retired sergeant-major of an MC wants to offload a few prizes. I doubt if it ever came within the musical experience of the Waltz King to save up 'Tales from a Vienna Wood' for the climax of the evening, only to have some twit unleash a netful of balloons from the ceiling right in the middle of it.

You may say that attacking balloons like wild beasts falling on sacrificial prey has profound Freudian undertones—

frustrated bosom-complex, perhaps, or birth-reenactment. You might even add fashionably '. . . that's what it's all about,' which brings us right back to the Hokey Cokey and not a moment too soon. I have a simpler explanation. Bursting balloons, like putting your right arm in and shaking it all about or weaving in and out of the gents' cloakroom in a crocodile, is just another excuse devised by the English to get out of dancing. We hate it, and it's about time we faced the fact. Look at that couple prancing past the bandstand, faces set in concentration, bristling like a hat-stand with elbows and teeth, doing the 'Come Dancing' bit for all they're worth. Oh, they're having fun all right, but it's the sort of fun that people get from running round the park before breakfast or swimming in the sea on Boxing Day. It's good exercise and it makes you feel jolly fit afterwards. Or observe that amorphous mass of hair over in the corner, twitching and shuddering with African rhythms. Their 'Top of the Pops' gyrations reflect a communal approach to life and the break-up of enclosed relationships in that nobody seems to be actually dancing *with* anyone. You just get out there and do your thing in the direction of anyone who happens to be looking. But it's more demo than dancing.

As for the rest, they're just walking round or leaning against each other, idly passing the time until some specific word of command galvanises them into action. Playing at political get-togethers, I am always relieved to see the local MP or prospective candidate hurry away to more urgent business before the dancing has really got under way. It might put altogether unhealthy ideas into his head to see how easily an English crowd, softened up and tortured into submission by dancing, can be driven into violent, uniform action by 'The March of the Mods' or 'Knees up Mother Brown'. It doesn't take an advanced course in demagogy to realise that, if you can get a man to put his right leg in and shake it all about, you can get him to do anything.

The seeds of jazz criticism—of which enough has been amassed over four decades to build a paper causeway between Calais and New Orleans—were sown in the early 'twenties when a plump youth called Hugues Panassié squeezed into the ventilation system of an expensive Paris hotel to overhear a negro band. He emerged with the solos of the black trumpeter Tommy Ladnier ringing in his ears and set about writing a book called *Le Jazz Hot*.

The story, which is probably untrue, is nonetheless reassuring, as it suggests that, before becoming a critic with all the weighty pontificating which that role entails, the late Monsieur Panassié had been an Ardent Fan. Being an Ardent Fan demands more than just unbridled enthusiasm. There must be the sort of dedication that calls for hard work, self-sacrifice and the spirit of an explorer of remote and dangerous parts. Hugues exemplified the last quality absolutely—it can have been no fun in that ventilator shaft with a chill breeze blowing up his trouser-legs and the possibility that, shimmying and wobbling rather too energetically to a hot chorus of *Shimme-Sha-Wobble*, he might have become irrevocably stuck, with unspeakable consequences to us all.

The first quality, that of sheer hard work, brings to mind that young man, invariably wearing the wooden, staring expression of an incurable fanatic, who comes backstage after band shows carrying an enormous volume which he shoves under your nose for inspection and signature. It contains the photographs of every act which has appeared at the Winter Gardens, Upper Spagforth-on-Sea (or wherever you happen to be) since Armistice Day 1918 and ranges indiscriminately over every conceivable musical presentation from Apache Bands, Musical Saw Specialists, All-Female Aggregations and Child Accordeonists to the better known bands of today and yesteryear. Over, alongside, under and sometimes right across each photograph is scrawled a signature, usually with a message of affection or esteem—'To our good friend Ron . . .' or 'With sincerest good wishes . . .'—which suggest that Ron has far more than his fair share of sincere and devoted friends, especially for a fellow whose conversation centres around what Jack Payne said to his Dad in 1936. Clearly the heavier of these volumes have been handed down from father to son, probably in a small but moving ceremony in which toasts are drunk to the memory of Rita Martino and her All-Ladies Gypsy Trombone Ensemble or the Eight Anstruthers (Seven Banjoes and a Song). Social historians, and students of dentistry through the ages, would find enough useless information in these vast bibles to keep them scribbling away for years, but Ardent Fans tend to inhabit a private world that cares nothing for posterity or indeed monetary gain.

One of the most hard-working fans I ever knew is the man, well known to any band that toured the Lincolnshire area in the early 'fifties, who turned up at every dance in the district carrying his own conductor's baton. It was sometimes rather confusing for bands who took their own conductor along with them to have extra-curricular direction and alternative time-keeping from a flailing figure right in front of the bandstand, but it showed enthusiasm and kept him extraordinarily fit.

The quality of self-sacrifice so necessary in an Ardent Fan is best exemplified in a personal story. Years ago, after a band tour in Switzerland, some of us stayed over in Paris for a night, intent on hearing some of the music which was then concentrated there. At the Vieux Colombier, where we heard Sidney Bechet, our limited funds were severely dented by a bad miscalculation. There was no admission fee, but you had to buy a drink inside. We thought that self-denial and a couple of Cokes each would see us through. It was only when the bill came up that we realised that the wily Gaul had outsmarted us. Coca-Cola was priced at the equivalent of twelve shillings a glass and it would have been cheaper to drink cognac. The setback left us just enough for a snack and we were famished.

Wandering in search of a café, we passed another club and saw the name of the American saxophone star Don Byas outside. We ascertained from the doorman that the same system applied and calculated that we could just afford the obligatory drink if we didn't eat. Providence clearly smiled upon our dedication for, at the table where we sat down inside, someone had just eaten and had left behind a plate of white bread and butter. We hid the plate underneath the table while the waiter cleared up, then ordered our drinks—and a bottle of meat sauce. As French meals go, the bread and butter spread with acrid brown sauce fell short of *Cordon Bleu*, but the music was delicious.

One prominent trait of the Ardent Fan is an inexhaustible curiosity. Round about the time that Hugues Panassié was bringing forth *Le Jazz Hot*, his close friend and associate Charles Delaunay was performing another inestimable service to humanity, inventing a new word in the process. His book, *Hot Discographie*, attempted, like a sort of Wisden's Almanack of jazz, to list every single record ever made, with details about dates, reference numbers and, most important of all, the musicians who played on each record. No Ardent Fan nowadays is without a discography in his bookshelves, from which, in these sophisticated times, he can find out exactly who played clarinet on the first (rejected) take of Louis 'Loose-leg' Braganza's *Loose Leg Stomp* recorded in Denver, Colorado on May 18th 1925 and not, as previously thought, in Richmond, Indiana on June 5th.

The greatest status symbol a musician can have is his own personal discographer. Mine, I add nonchalantly, is a distinguished heart-surgeon in Glasgow who, in the moments when he is not repairing holes-in-the-heart, diligently fills in the gaps in my vital statistics. He is also a generous host to musicians who travel North. We once spent several hours together slaving over innumerable giant whiskies in order to work out who, on one of my recordings, shouts 'Yeah!' in the third bar of the trumpet solo. At one stage in my career I began to get rather worried at the persistence with which he recommended me to have a routine chest X-ray up at his hospital. It was only after I acquiesced that I discovered the real reason for his concern. He wanted a blueprint of my insides for his discographical files.

American musicians coming to Europe have always been astonished, and sometimes dismayed, to find that every fan-in-the-street has a sort of data bank on his recording activities in the distant past. It may be this ruthless investigatory zeal that has made some visiting jazzmen of advanced age adopt evasive or even sealed-lips tactics towards their admirers.

During a season by the late Coleman Hawkins at Ronnie Scott's Club in London, I was sitting with Ben Webster one night when Hawkins came up to join us. The relationship between the two great American tenor-saxists was one of master and pupil and Ben, though a master in his own right, clearly held the older man in some awe. Certainly Coleman Hawkins, with his baleful eye and straggly, Jomo Kenyatta beard, was a formidable old lion for whom the youthful nickname 'Bean' had become quite inappropriate. The two men sat exchanging casual badinage until an aristocratic-looking Englishman approached, elegant wife in tow. The man introduced himself as Lord Someone-or-other, presented his wife and reminded Ben that they had met fleetingly before. 'I wonder,' he said, 'if you would do us the great honour of introducing us to Mr. Hawkins.' Ben Webster duly obliged, the couple sat down next to Hawkins, and there descended upon our little group a fathomless and seemingly eternal silence. It was eventually broken by Ben in what he seemed to imagine was a confidential whisper for my ears alone. 'Ever'body waitin' for Bean to talk,' he bellowed. Then, even louder '. . . he ain't gonna talk!!!' And talk he didn't.

Yes, being an Ardent Fan can be bruising to the ego. One can imagine the discomfiture of the affluent diner in the prewar

Everybody waitin' for Bean to talk....

Coleman Hawkins

Mayfair Hotel who sent up to the late Bert Ambrose a request wrapped in a one-pound note—and seconds later got back the answer 'We don't play requests,' wrapped up in a fiver!

Sometimes actual physical danger is involved. Graeme Bell's Australian Jazz Band toured here in the early 'fifties with a line in Public Relations which didn't exclude a little pugilism when the occasion demanded. There used to be a ballroom in Glasgow called Barrowlands where, as the curtains parted, the visiting band was confronted with the reassuring sight of a row of massive 'chuckers-out' standing shoulder to shoulder in front of the stand *and facing the audience.* The Bell boys heeded with relish and some involuntary clenching of the fists the warning that, quite often, Glaswegians bent upon expressing themselves in direct action would evade the bodyguard and commit mayhem among the music stands.

In the event, their session at Barrowlands started disconcertingly quietly. Apart from an occasional wild cry and the sound of shattering glass from the body of the hall, no kind of fun seemed to be brewing. Then, at the height of the evening, Graeme Bell himself, seated at the piano, saw in the corner of his eye a figure mount the stage and approach him from behind. With an exultant Antipodean roar he leapt up and, without pausing, let fly with a wild right-hander. An autograph book flew in one direction, a pencil in the other, and a bespectacled young man who, up until the moment of impact had been an Ardent Fan, lay spread-eagled on the dance floor. It was his own fault. He should have stuck to the ventilator shaft, like Hugues Panassié.

Distinguished Visitors

Distinguished Visitors

'WENT TO THE SAVOY to hear the new American saxophone-player . . .' Substitute 'Ronnie Scott's' for the Savoy and the sentence could well come from a contemporary jazz fan's letter home. It does in fact appear in Arnold Bennett's Diary, entered in 1924. Bennett goes on to record that the saxophone-player in question kept a pet bird in a cage beside him on the stand, which shows that the tradition for mild eccentricity among visiting American musicians stretches back several decades before the day of Thelonious Monk and Rahsaan Roland Kirk.

But the real interest in Arnold Bennett's entry lies in the innocent word 'American' in this context. For 1924 was indeed a time when the personnels of London dance bands, with their Harrys and Freddys and Syds, were enlivened by such unmistakably transatlantic names as Sylvester Ahola, Chelsea Quealey, Al Starita and Fud Livingstone. Several quite disparate events conspired to alter the status of the American musicians in Britain and Europe. First, the Wall Street crash sent many of them scurrying home to take charge of family affairs. Then a trade dispute between the musicians' unions of Britain and America put a ban on the casual exchange of musicians between the two countries. And most important of all, Monsieur Hugues Panassié of France had written his book *Le Jazz Hot* and, in passing, invented an institution called ze 'Ot Cloob.

Under the guidance—some might say the Papal decree—of M. Panassié and his central 'Ot Cloob de France, 'Ot Cloobs all over Europe spread the word that anyone who had ever been remotely connected with a jazz band in America was a 'grande vedette' or big star. To be able to put the words 'Jazz' and 'Americain' together on a poster, especially with the suffix 'noir', was to ensure ecstatic crowds and a certain amount of mayhem around the box office.

Very soon the French liner *Île de France* had assumed a role almost as important in jazz history as those Mississippi boats that took jazz up-river from New Orleans to Chicago. On every transatlantic trip she brought over at least one American musician who was delighted to find himself received like royalty.

I am happy to say that we in Britain held ourselves somewhat aloof from these hysterical goings-on. For one thing, we had our Musicians' Union to protect our interests by keeping all American musicians out between 1935 and 1956. Then we wisely rejected ze 'Ot Cloob as being an unreliable Froggy institution, redolent of inefficiency and garlic. Instead, we had Rhythm Clubs, which are rather easier to pronounce with a stiff upper lip. Furthermore, we do not as a nation go in much for treating people as royalty. We have our own royalty, thank you, and we don't even treat them as royalty.

For all these reasons, American jazz musicians have tended, until very recently to remain tourists in this country rather than residents. Some have outdone the tourists in their reaction to our institutions. Bud Freeman, tenor-saxist of the tough Chicago school, had been a life-long Anglophile, modelling his appearance on Ronald Colman and punctuating rugged bursts of saxophone-playing with quotations from Shakespeare.

When he first made it to this country in 1963, it was for a special festival run by, among others, Lord Montague of Beaulieu and the Hon. Gerald Lascelles, the Queen's cousin. Picked up at the airport in a vast, peacock-blue, chauffeur-driven limousine and transported past the silhouettes of Eton Collège Chapel and Windsor Castle to Fort Belvedere, Bud was in ecstasy when I met him at a Press reception on the sweeping lawn. 'Humphrey,' he said, 'you've no idea what this means to me. England is just as I always imagined it.'

In the early thirties, when jazz visits had become commonplace, our Royalty had to get used to a certain absence of protocol when confronted by the jazz aristocracy. George V, who seems to have been quite a jazz buff in his own quiet way, must have felt a twinge of astonishment when, at a Command Performance, young Louis Armstrong unleashed a red-hot trumpet solo at him with the words 'This one's for you, Rex!'

Around the same time, Lord Beaverbrook gave a party for the then Prince of Wales at which the visiting Duke Ellington band played the music. The Duke of York, later George VI, asked Duke Ellington to do a solo of *Swampy River* which was in the royal record collection. Ellington didn't recognise him and gave him what he later described as 'the light fluff'. It wasn't George VI's night. Later the band left to go on to a recording studio, taking many of the guests with them. But the Scotland Yard detective wouldn't let him go because of the crush. For some reason the Prince of Wales got through the security net and, at some stage when, alas, the record machine wasn't operating, sat in on drums. As Duke Ellington recalled, 'We expected some Little Lord Fauntleroy stuff but he really gave out with some lowdown Charleston'. As the Charleston went out of fashion some ten years earlier, we may draw our own conclusions.

My own recollection of the old European jazz scene in all its splendid absurdity centres upon a concert in Paris in the late fifties. It was held in the vast Palais des Sports, where they used to end the six-day bicycle race. The star of the concert was, by a delicious irony, the man who, on a first visit to France in 1929,

101

had put Hugues Panassié straight about jazz—the self-confessed one-time opium-smoker, small-time gangster, dope-peddler and clarinetist, Mezz Mezzrow. While the capacity audience blew whistles and shook rattles upstairs, fifteen bands, comprising upwards of a hundred and fifty musicians, were marshalled by hysterical stewards in the concrete passages below, in order to emerge from below ground in an opening parade.

It is impossible to describe the din when, in the echoing, pipe-lined labyrinth under the stadium, we struck up at a given signal with 'High Society.' Mezzrow set off at the head of the procession with a steward steering him at each elbow. They went too fast and disappeared from sight, at which point those following took a wrong turning and led us all into a cul-de-sac, playing 'High Society' and swearing alternately. Responding to cries of 'Turn back' in six different languages, a bass drummer at the rear did a military countermarch and got himself stuck sideways-on in the narrow passage trapping us all. While an inferno raged beneath, Mezz Mezzrow in the meantime had reached the steps leading up into the auditorium. Piping away manfully on the clarinet, he emerged, not at the head of a triumphant parade, but entirely alone.

Anywhere else in the world it would have been a grotesque anticlimax. But it seemed that the massed 'Ot Cloobs of the entire universe were there, fully-primed. Hitler arriving in the Nuremberg Stadium never knew the ovation that they gave the solitary Mezzrow that night.

Since those early days, improvement in, and recognition for, British jazz has led to collaboration on a more equal basis, and many of my happiest memories are of tours with, and alongside American jazzmen.

Buck

WHEN BUCK CLAYTON toured with my band in the early sixties, he made it clear from the outset that he didn't want to work as a 'star' soloist but as a member of the band. Before his first tour, he sent over some arrangements and compositions at my request, and I noticed that he had written himself second trumpet parts throughout. His reasons were a characteristic blend of politeness and practicality—as leader of the band I should have the first part, which would also ensure that we could continue to play the arrangements after he had left us. In view of the fact that the first parts were higher and more punishing, I'm not sure there wasn't a wrestler's trick lurking in there somewhere.

I must explain. In the course of working with American musicians I have discovered the fundamental difference between the British and American philosophy of life. The Briton maintains a stiff upper lip and says 'Never kick a man when he's down.' The American juts his jaw and says 'Always kick a man when he's down—it may be the last chance you'll get.' During one of Buck's tours with us we played at a big festival in Manchester, at which Dizzy Gillespie was also appearing as soloist with the John Dankworth Orchestra. In the finale, Buck was to join Dizzy and the orchestra in a last appearance. For reasons not wholly unconnected with over-indulgence on a grand scale,

Dizzy had incapacitated himself that night to the point where he really could not play at all. The familiar embouchure, bolstered by cheeks puffed up like aubergines, was drained of strength—a situation easily brought on by digestive overstrain, and dreaded by trumpet-players. Earlier in the festival, he had annoyed Buck by wandering on-stage and clowning during our set. When Buck joined Dizzy at the end of a set which had been, for everyone, a painful embarrassment, he was in tigerish form, playing so superbly that members of the Dankworth orchestra forgot their gentlemanly allegiance to their own guest and applauded him wildly. Afterwards, Buck denied having done a hatchet job on a defenceless Dizzy, but, consciously or not, the deed had been done.

On our concerts, Buck and I often engaged in trumpet exchanges. In range and stamina Buck had the edge on me most of the time. Nevertheless he would often murmur, 'Take it easy tonight, Humph—my chops are in poor shape', just before we embarked on our special trumpet duet called 'Me and `Buck'. As befits an Old Etonian and former officer in Her Majesty's First Regiment of Foot Guards, I behaved in a gentlemanly manner, avoiding any display of fireworks which might put my American friend at a disadvantage and dismissing all base suspicions when, invariably, his ailing chops made a dramatic recovery just as it was his turn to play. One night he went too far. We always ended our performances with Irving Berlin's 'The Song is Ended', over which I made the closing announcement. As the honoured guest Buck would play the final cadenza, climbing up to an impressive high F. At the Manchester Sports Guild, after a hard and hot session, he made the climb up to E and then turned and pointed to me. Unprepared, the lips relaxed after playing a second part in the low register, I had to hit a high F out of the blue. In the agonised rush of wind there was a high F somewhere to be heard but it was more of a cry for help than a musical note.

After that I openly accused Buck of playing wrestler's tricks—that is to say, feigning weakness and incapacity until his opponent relaxed and then leaping in with a paralysing half-Nelson. He laughed a lot at the suggestion but didn't actually deny it. A few nights later he whispered, as I called our duet, 'Take it easy on me tonight, Humph—I left my jock-strap back in the hotel.' Jock strap or no, I played flat out. Since those days, our firm friendship has been cemented on a keen mutual awareness of wrestler's tricks (we recorded an original tune with that title). Some years ago, Buck suffered a cruel series of illnesses which forced him to stop playing. It was inconceivable that the close association with the band built up in the 'sixties should cease, so, when I heard that he was beginning to turn his attention to writing, I commissioned some compositions from him which we eventually recorded with Buddy Tate as guest and tenor-saxist. When I glanced through them and saw that Buck had designated me to play first clarinet in a number at breakneck speed, I knew that he had not packed the wrestler's tricks away with his horn. I play clarinet slowly, in one key.

As men who had had to make their own way in the world with stiff competition from all comers, jazz musicians tend to develop a Machiavellian sense of humour. Buck was never happier, when we drove round the country together, than when I recounted disasters that involved his American friends and colleagues—how Henry Allen and my band had a row onstage in Manchester, and how Ben Webster was ejected by the police from the Nottingham club where he was appearing as star soloist, and asked the young policeman who had him in an armlock, 'Did you ever know Art Tatum?' Ben Webster was part-Red Indian and, below a certain specific gravity, the sweetest man who ever walked. When flash level was reached, he developed a suicidal tendency to attack anyone in official uniform. Stories of Ben ending a foray with a squad of policemen or hotel night staff sitting on his protesting head would always get the

Ben Webster

same gleeful but affectionate response from Buck, 'Yeah, that's Ben.'

As a part-Indian himself, Buck has always asserted that 'Indians always fight when they get drunk.' I never knew Buck himself get more than mildly grumpy, though he told of an epic fight in his Basie band youth with fellow-trumpeter Ed Lewis which took place on a sidewalk after a small difference of opinion and lasted 45 minutes until they were both arrested. When Buck woke up in jail next morning the first thing he saw was a shoe wedged in the bars of the cell window.

Pee Wee Russell was another Indian with whom Buck often worked. With Pee Wee, youthful saturation as a drinking companion to Bix Beiderbecke (whom he survived miraculously by almost forty years) had led in abstemious middle-age to a permanent state of what Buck called 'grouchiness'. Many times I had to retell to an eager Buck Clayton the story of Pee Wee's interview with Steve Allen, one of the producers of a BBC jazz programme. Steve used to compile a feature called 'Hear me talkin'', in which visiting jazzmen talked about their lives in music and chose a few records—a sort of miniature 'Desert Island Discs'. One day he went to Pee Wee's London hotel room, to interview him. He knocked on the door. 'Who's that?' 'Steve Allen from the BBC.' 'O.K., c'mon in.' Inside, Steve outlined what the programme was about. When he got to the point about choosing four or five records, Pee Wee said, 'Hold it! I can't do that. How do I know what are the best five records. I haven't heard 'em all.' Steve explained that it didn't have to be the *best* five records—any records would do. But Pee Wee was adamant—he was in no position to choose the best five records. After a long argument at cross purposes, Steve was driven to sarcasm. 'Mr. Russell, do you think it would be best if I went outside and we started all over again?' 'Yes,' said Pee Wee. So Steve went out into the corridor and knocked. 'Who's that?' 'Steve Allen from the BBC.' 'O.K., c'mon in.' Inside again,

Steve went through the whole outline of the programme, reaching the point about choosing five records. 'Hold it!' said Pee Wee. . . .

Only once did I personally suffer from Buck's relish for catastrophe. I was briefed to organise a concert at the Royal Festival Hall which, in addition to my own band and two British rhythm sections, was to star five visiting Americans—Buck Clayton, Ben Webster, Ruby Braff, the cornetist, Vic Dickenson, the trombonist, and Big Joe Turner. I decided to split the instrumentalists into small groups, adding Bruce Turner to make up one of the front-lines. On the way back from a gig the night before I told Buck my plans. When I talked of putting Vic and Ruby together with Bruce in one group, Buck's only response was a low chuckle. Had I said something funny? 'No, it's nothing,' said Buck, chuckling again. I pressed him. 'Well, it's just that when I last saw Vic he said that never again in his *life* would he work with Ruby.' 'Oh,' I said. Then I told him that I would like him to appear with Ben and Vic. This time it was more of a belly-laugh than a chuckle. 'Don't tell me you won't work with them!' I cried. 'Hell, no,' he said, 'but when Ben and Vic last worked together in the States, they ended up having a fight. Boy, did they *fight*!!'

I have never liked The Royal Festival Hall. Every performer has a jinx place that makes him nervous, and for me, the Festival Hall is it. I once used to have a recurring nightmare before every appearance there. In it the hall was roofless under a blue sky. At the back of the furthest stalls was a Dali-esque viaduct and beyond it more audience stretched away to hazy infinity. When I went onstage before this vast audience I found that all I could do was hum through the trumpet as if it were a kazoo. While I hummed inaudibly the audience, all ten million of them, would get up one by one and walk out. And I would wake up sweating—and humming. Before the all-star concert in question I spent an entirely sleepless night, thanks to Buck.

There was nothing I could do about altering the programme—when I had suggested putting Ben on with Ruby, Buck nearly fell out of the car.

As it turned out, I could have slept like a baby. When they arrived at the Festival Hall for rehearsal, the Americans fell into each other's arms in great brotherly embraces. In the ever-open backstage bar all was sweetness and light and at least one can say that the concert made up in camaraderie what it lacked in coherence. When I announced Ben Webster's re-appearance for the finale and was told, in stentorian whispers from the wings, that he had gone home, I felt thankful for small mercies. At least he hadn't attacked an official.

Big Joe

I HAVE NOTICED that Americans give a special meaning to the word 'style'. When someone once rather naively invited a member of Louis Armstrong's six-piece All Stars out for a meal and suggested that he bring along some of the other musicians, the answer was 'I don't run with those cats—they're not my style.'

Buck and Big Joe Turner, who toured together with us in 1965, were a contrast in style. Buck Clayton was remarkably handsome even, as he was then, in his middle fifties, with the unique blue eyes lending to his face the alert yet sensuous look of a cat. He has always chosen his clothes with care, sporting in one phase of his British visits an English look complete with waistcoat and bowler hat, in which he looked superb. Always the courtly ladies' man, he liked to make for sophisticated nightspots after his work was done, making many friends outside the circle of musicians and fans who surrounded him wherever he played.

Big Joe Turner was, by comparison, an innocent. By the time he came to work with us, the longstanding prefix 'Big' had come to denote more than his considerable height. He was by then Vast Joe Turner, so massive in girth that when he bought a sports jacket at the specialist Big Man's shop on the Edgware

Road they had to insert a lanyard with a button at each end to bring it together across his middle. It was hard at first sight to reconcile the huge, genial man with his eager boy's face and rather worried, insecure temperament with that forthright voice, full of masculine assertiveness, that belted out penetrating and quite sophisticated blues lyrics of his own devising on so many cherished records.

On one of our early journeys out of town we pulled up at some traffic lights alongside a radio shop. 'Man,' said Joe to Buck, 'I'd like to get me one of them little English radios to take home.' 'Why, you can get radios like that anywhere in the States,' Buck pointed out. 'Yeah,' said Joe, 'but I sure like the programmes they get.' On another occasion he announced, as we passed a gardening shop, 'I think I'll take home one of those lawn-mowers.' The prospect of Joe, encumbered already with a hold-all the size and weight of a rolled-up rhinoceros, checking in at Heathrow with a lawn-mower reduced Buck and me to a stunned silence. 'Yeah,' mused Joe, 'I'm gonna be the only guy in my street who has a lawn-mower with an English accent!' Here we were getting a little closer to the blues man whose original line of thought had introduced such contemporary 'props' of T.V. and RADAR into his lyrics.

Fortunately the logistics of exporting a lawn-mower eventually deterred him. He was not a man for meeting the complexities of life half way. Once he got me to stop the car on the outskirts of Manchester. He had spotted a camera shop and wanted to buy a camera—'I don't want one of them complicated things, just sump'n' I can put up to my eye and shoot.' I conveyed this wish to the salesman, who showed him the newest thing in instant automatic cameras. Halfway through the explanation about cartridge-loading, self-focusing, automatic exposure and fool-proof wind-on, Joe took fright: 'Man, you gotta go to *school* to work this!' he cried as he beat a lumbering retreat.

111

Buck treated Joe with affectionate indulgence and occasional incredulity. Whenever we went into a roadside store for refreshment, Joe, whose almost consonant-free dialect was hard enough to understand at the best of times, would confuse the person behind the sweet counter even more by asking for a 'soda pop'. Buck shook his head in wonderment. 'You know, back home I never heard anyone talk about a soda-pop for *thirty years*!' It was only when Joe's dependence on Buck intruded upon the latter's social life that things became a little strained. Joe, who wore his trilby hat squarely on the back of his head and sported a huge camel-hair coat that reached down to his massive ankles, hardly fitted in with Buck's nocturnal plans, and there was a hint of exasperation in Buck's voice when he described how, night after night, he would tiptoe, dressed to kill, past Joe's hotel door only to hear it open as he passed to reveal Joe, trilby and top-coat already on, asking 'Where we goin' tonight, Buck?'

In matters of low finance, too, Joe often took on the role of innocent abroad. On his very first night here we went to Annie's Room, Annie Ross's short-lived night club. Outside in Russell St., we were approached by one of those down-and-outs who materialise, when you are quite successfully parking your car, to encumber you with help. Joe reached into his pocket to reward him for his antics, but I assured him it wasn't necessary. After a festive hour or two during which Buck and Joe both sat in with Annie and the band, we emerged to find the self-appointed attendant still there, now weaving and lurching even more obviously. This time there was no deterring Joe. As the man touched his cap and bobbed obsequiously, Joe put his hand into his trouser pocket, scooped out a fistful of loose change amounting on my reckoning to several pounds and deposited the lot in the man's hastily outstretched hand.

A week or two later we did a television programme from a studio in Westbourne Grove. In the pub nearby at lunchtime

we were entertained by an amateur folk-group. Towards the end of their set a girl came round with a pint glass collecting contributions. I put in a coin and then said to her, 'Go straight to that big man in the corner—I think you'll get a pleasant surprise.' Buck and I watched as she spoke to Joe. We couldn't see exactly what happened, but we guessed. The girl came back, her glass brimming with assorted coins. 'Gosh!' she said, 'you were right—but don't you think I should give some back? He emptied both pockets and it looks like about £8!' We told her not to bother.

Onstage, Joe Turner occasionally showed the insecurity which seemed to dog his incursions into unfamiliar surroundings. He sang almost every one of his blues and standard pop songs in the key of C. It became a matter of reflex action for us to lead into an introduction in C. Having done so for about six nights in a row, it was not unusual for us to hear Joe, on the seventh night, lamenting, 'Wrong key, wrong key!' as soon as we started. He had a stock phrase, a hangover from the rhyming hip jargon of the 'forties, to express his periodical—and always unfounded—conviction that things had gone wrong. 'We're in a world of trouble,' he would cry, 'Someone took a pin and busted the bubble!' But when he was confident and in congenial company, the big penetrating voice assumed an air of massive authority.

To some listeners over here, weaned on rock 'n roll and theatrically extrovert 'rhythm 'n blues', his manner of delivery, standing foursquare with the huge frame bent forward slightly and little movement beyond the snapping of finger and thumb, was disappointingly short of frenetic, as was his limiting of his vocal range for the most part to four of five notes. They missed the passionate intensity which lay beneath the repetitive phrases and the dramatic effect achieved when, by changing just one beautifully-judged note, he gave a stanza an unexpected emotional jolt. Joe Turner, the singer of powerful, sexually-assertive, sometimes quite cynical blues ('baby you're so beautiful but you've gotta die someday') personifies for me the jazz fan's perennial problem—how to reconcile two often irreconcilable halves of a musician, his music and his overt personality. For me there are still two Joe Turners, and I love them both.

Hip music, Square screen

A GOOD OPPORTUNITY to watch a great range of American jazz musicians in action came when I was booked to introduce the BBC 2 series of jazz programmes, called respectively 'Jazz 625' and 'Jazz Goes to College.' It was a less nerve-wracking experience than I expected in the light of the great variety of temperaments to which, as the 'front man' of the shows, I was exposed. Significantly, the only musician who was arrogantly unpleasant and obstructive was an organist of relatively minor talent. The rest of us worked together amicably, if not always smoothly.

The hardest problem facing the producer, Terry Henebery, was to persuade the musicians that, to achieve a good sound balance, it was necessary to have some rehearsal. Naturally enough, the musicians who had often been rushed to the studio straight from London Airport or from some distant concert venue, were more concerned with energy conservation. When Thelonious Monk, for instance, arrived to record his programme at the Cambridge Union on a hot summer's day, he responded to Terry's request for a run-through of one number by playing a single chorus, in old-fashioned 'stride' style, of 'Lulu's Back in Town' and then walking purposefully towards the door. 'We'll need a little more than that!' said Terry via the floor manager with the slightest touch of sarcasm. Expressionless, Monk returned to the piano and played 'Lulu's Back in Town' through again, just once. This time he was out of the door and beyond reach before anyone could stop him.

As compére I went into the recording (of two programmes) with very little idea of what was going to happen. Fortunately, my hot-seat, from which I was to introduce the music in a relaxed and knowledgeable manner, was just under the end of the rostrum where Charlie Rouse, the tenor-saxist, was standing. Charlie and I had been friends ever since we toured with Monk's Quartet in America, and he came to my rescue with a steady flow of information in between his own solos.

On TV, the job of passing on a producer's instructions and requests to the set normally belongs to the floor-manager, an authoritative type permanently encased in head-phones who, because he is partially insulated against the sound of his own voice, tends to issue instructions in a barrack-square bellow. Stentorian injunctions like 'Hold it, Squire, HOLD IT!!' or 'Start again, old son!!' directed at jazzmen of uncertain temperament in the full flood of creation added considerable suspense to rehearsals, and I quite often had to step in as interpreter.

When Sonny Rollins did a show at Reading University, it was a case of *not* stepping in. We had a floor-manager there who had just been promoted to the job and was doing his first show. Max Roach's Quintet shared the bill with Rollins, and Max had already unnerved the poor young man with one or two temperamental skirmishes. The format of the recording, which was before an audience of students, was that each band was to be introduced by me and, on a cue from the floor-manager, would play about two minutes of music over which the titles could eventually be run, after which I would make the opening announcement into the show. We got through Max Roach's set without a hitch, the floor-manager willingly leaving it to me to signal the cues to Max. After a short break we set about recording Sonny Rollins for the second programme.

Sonny is one of the most remarkable improvisers in all of jazz. At Ronnie Scott's, where he was currently appearing, he used to remain in his dressing-room while Ronnie introduced him and then literally come out playing, starting his theme as he made his way to the stand and then improvising without break for anything between forty-five minutes and an hour. In this time he would pass from one tune to another, linking theme and variation in an astonishing stream of consciousness and sometimes dipping into an uncannily retentive memory to pick up a phrase which had occurred some minutes earlier.

Taking one look at Sonny's broad-shouldered, monolithic stature and that striking chieftain's face, our floor-manager at Reading took fright—unreasonably, as Sonny is the gentlest of men. At the end of the break between sets, Terry Henebery told me to bring the musicians on-stage while he made his way back to the control-van outside. I introduced each musician to the audience. When I came to 'Ladies and Gentlemen, Sonny Rollins!', Sonny started to play. The theme was his own piece, 'St. Thomas', with which he used to open at Ronnie Scott's. After several bars, high-pitched sounds of protest and consternation escaped from the floor-manager's headphones, indicating that Terry Henebery had reached the control-box and found that everything had started without him. The floor-manager looked aghast and turned to me. 'He wants me to stop him!' he said, in a voice of horror. Then, pleading, 'Will you do it?' I gave the matter a moment's thought and then said, 'Suggest to Terry from me that we let it go on and record an opening bit afterward—that way we know we'll get some good music whereas if we interrupt to flow we might get none.'

It proved to be the wisest choice, for Sonny played superbly without a stop for forty-five minutes. At the end of it, Terry sent in a message asking him to play a short two-minute piece as an opener. I got as far as saying 'We'd like a little bit more . . .'

when Sonny started up again and played for another three-quarters of an hour. I never saw the finished programme so I don't know how Terry solved the details of presentation. But I am certain that whatever that floor-manager has done since, be it anything from student riots to Monty Python, has seemed a piece of cake!

There were, during that series of TV programmes, quite a few minor mishaps. The New Orleans veteran Henry 'Red' Allen made the mistake of visiting a Chinese restaurant during the dinner-break, and was brought to a halt in the middle of his solo coda in 'Rosetta' by a treacherous grain of fried rice which had been lurking behind a back tooth and shot into his trumpet mouthpiece at exactly the wrong moment. Big Joe Turner, appearing with my band, heard me announce 'How Long Blues' and became convinced that I had made a mistake. 'Wrong tune, wrong tune!' he cried, 'We're in a world of trouble!' So he sang 'Cherry Red' instead, which he had already sung not ten minutes earlier. Stan Getz and Astrud Gilberto, billed to appear together on the strength of their hit-making bossa-nova partnership, arrived tight-lipped and tearful respectively, having reached the point of irrevocable break-up that very day. So they had to record separate shows.

One programme only never saw the light of day, and that was not through any failure to film it. The late Albert Ayler was then the most talked-of exponent of what has been variously called 'free form', 'avant-garde' or the 'new' jazz. He was recorded at the London School of Economics and his arrival aroused great suspense and intrigued expectancy among London fans and musicians, especially as a hassle at London Airport delayed it by several hours. The musicians arrived tired, angry and bristling with aggression, insisting on refreshment before they would play a note. So they were directed to the students' canteen, for which, after what seemed an exorbitant length of time, a message came down that some delay and confusion was being caused by Donald Ayler, Albert's brother and trumpeter with the band, who was standing on his head in the self-service queue, presumably to achieve relaxation. There was a scuffle when the queue became restive and only the diplomatic intervention of a road manager prevented the entire cast of the evening's performance being ejected from the building.

When we eventually came to recording a programme, there were one or two technical hitches which did nothing to lower the tension. The third member of the front-line was a Belgian violinist, alleged to be a successful concert performer in his own country. On this occasion he performed a caricature impression of an anti-social, alienated 'modern jazz' musician with a chip on the shoulder, storming off-stage with mumbled curses whenever things went wrong. The whole episode was for me, as a bystander who kept out of things as much as possible, richly entertaining.

In the audience were many British musicians of the 'modern' school who took more violent exception to the music than some of the entrenched traditionalists. After one of the technical hold-ups, the floor-manager addressed the audience: 'We must apologise for interrupting the music once again.' 'WHY?' shouted the voice of Ronnie Scott from the auditorium. And pianist Gordon Beck was heard enquiring the whereabouts of Covent Garden fruit-market so that he could get ammunition to hurl at the stage.

The music itself was a strange mixture of hymn-like dirges, played in rough union with a bleating, street-band sound which I found not unattractive, and those frenetic bursts of musical gibberish which have come to be known as 'freakouts'. At the time I had engaged in many arguments with musicians of 'avant-garde' persuasion about the musical validity of these outbursts of cacophony. One frequent justification was they were the logical extension of emotion—that players, playing either solo or collectively, build their improvisations to such a pitch of excitement that to shriek is the only way of releasing it. Fair enough, I used to say, adding the modest proviso that I would rather not be around when it happened. Then Albert Ayler came, and while I stood in the wings eager to learn, blew the 'spontaneous emotion' theory sky-high. After stubbornly resisting Terry Henebery's request for two minutes of music to open the programme, Ayler eventually gave in and turned to the band. 'OK, guys—for two minutes we go crazy.' And they did.

Now Albert Ayler is dead, and his role in the development of contemporary jazz has yet to be determined. The men upstairs at the BBC took one look at the programme which we recorded at the L.S.E. and decided that it was not suitable for transmission. A year or two later, in an act of criminal negligence, almost all the irreplaceable stock of BBC 2 jazz recordings—perhaps the most comprehensive collection of 'in action' jazz recordings in the world—were wiped off in a routine exercise to conserve video-tape. When the British jazz fraternity discovered the act of vandalism, it went crazy for a good deal longer than two minutes!

Coals to Newcastle

IN THE AUTUMN of 1959 my band made its first—and to date, only—trip to the United States. I can't say that I took to America on sight. For one thing, New York was enjoying one of its autumnal bouts of humidity and when we stepped out of the plane it was like walking straight into a warm, damp blanket. For the three days before we left on tour life beyond the range of an air-conditioner was very uncomfortable. Naturally we spent most nights exploring the jazz spots, so fatigue was added to discomfort. By day there was a certain amount of hustling—interviews with journalists, one or two radio shows and so on.

When the temperature was at its highest I had to go with the tour promoter Jay Weston, to meet a newspaperman from *Time* Magazine in a smart bar somewhere around Fifth Avenue. When I walked in without a jacket a manager came across and said sorry, but I couldn't stay in the bar in that state of undress. After some discussion he agreed to lend me a lightweight jacket. It took some time for him and Jay between them to manipulate my fifteen-stone frame into a white jacket which seemed to belong to a slender boy of twelve. While the wrestling was going on I asked the man rather testily why a jacket was compulsory. 'Why, if we didn't have the rule, all kinds of rough people could

122

just walk in off the sidewalk.' 'Oh,' I said and sat down, looking in my boy's jacket like something that had fallen off a garbage truck en route from Bums' Alley.

Broadway was a disappointment. From all those popular songs I had envisaged a sort of theatrical Champs Elysées, and the quite narrow and, by day, tatty street was a let-down.

The jazz haunts, on the other hand, were a jazz-fan's dream. At Birdland, now alas defunct, we heard Buddy Rich, Art Blakey, Maynard Ferguson—and we almost heard Miles Davis, whose Quintet was billed to appear but who had got involved in a birthday celebration for Ella Fitzgerald up at the bar and declined the piercing invitation of Pee-Wee Marquette, the club's diminutive emcee, to return to the stand for his second set. The Metropole was another place to be visited as soon as possible. Henry 'Red' Allen led the band there, towering majestically over the imbibing customers on the extraordinary bandstand which ranged along behind the bar. Sometimes in the daytime there was a Dixieland session led by an extrovert and gymnastic trombonist called Conrad Janis. We never went to one of those sessions. We didn't have to—if we opened our bedroom windows at the President Hotel three blocks away, we heard it all.

My favourite place was Basie's Bar, to which I was first taken by John Hammond one night after a delicious meal, seasoned with the music of Roy Eldridge, at a restaurant called the Allegro. Basie's was a long bar, not by any means large, with the band along one wall standing eyeball to eyeball with the customers perched at the bar counter. We went there several times, to enjoy the music of 'Sir Charles' Thompson's Trio and, when Jimmy Rushing was in our company, to join him in demolishing pork-chops provided by a massive lady beside whom Jim looked merely plump. They always told me that everything in America is much bigger and that certainly goes for the fatties.

It was at Basie's one night that Tony Coe borrowed a clarinet, sat in with the trio and had the cool Harlem bar-flies literally jumping with astonishment. English critics, both professional and amateur, suffer from a compulsion to compare or qualify whenever they are confronted with British jazz. 'Who does he sound like?' is the first thing they ask themselves, searching for some established American name against whom to measure the home product. The predominately black clientele at Basie's—not in those embryonic days of Black Power notably affectionate towards whites—expressed, in a sybillant and monosyllabic four-letter word that rustled from one end of the bar to the other, the unstinting view that, wherever Tony came from, here was one hell of a clarinet player.

Despite the joys of listening to so much jazz first-hand, I found New York a nervy, worrying place at first. Americans are the most delightfully courteous people in the world. Let's put it another way. Americans are the most abominably rude people in the world. Either will do. I am ready to hang a thousand persuasive words on each of those pegs. But for the moment, let's be content with an example or two.

Compare the behaviour of the Englishman and the American on entering a crowded lift. Thrown into close proximity with his fellow men, the Englishman looks as acutely miserable as a schoolboy who has just wet his trousers. He goes through the most elaborate routine to avoid communicating—peering intently at the roof, wiping an imaginary spot off his tie, reading the emergency instructions as though his immediate survival depended on it, humming a tuneless 'boom-boom-boom' to himself to ward off any approach from his fellow travellers. The American, on the other hand, greets the assembled company with 'Good morning' or whatever. It's not much, and it is often said with the dyspeptic and deeply melancholy expression of a man on the way to do a job for 'Legs' Diamond. But at least it is said.

The readiness to communicate with all-comers is one of the fruits of a virtually classless and protocol-free society. And the alleged rudeness of Americans springs from the same source. I can still recall the shock when I discovered that, as well as having no 'manners' themselves, the Americans actively resented mine.

On a particularly hot and humid autumn day when my sensitivity was already sharpened by the feeling that a wet St. Bernard was sitting on my head, I showed the hall porter at the President Hotel a mountain of band and personal baggage and asked with some diffidence if he would take the bags up to the rooms, please. He could not have taken more offence at the word 'please' if I had called him 'my man'. 'Sure I take the bags up!' he snapped, 'I'm the porter, ain't I?' Brought up to say please and thank you and to know just how much food to leave behind on my plate for Mr. Manners without at the same time depriving starving children in Russia, I found it hard to adapt. But adapt I did, and when we came back to the President Hotel after a three-week tour, my curt jerk of the thumb and 'Hey c'mon, feller, the bags!' regained his respect and persuaded him that I was not some kind of a fag. I think I even called him Mack.

As one who believes fervently that, for all of its shortcomings, Britain is in everyday matters the most quietly efficient country in the world, I do not subscribe to the myth that life in the U.S. runs like a hyper-effective supercharged machine. Our own tour was a catalogue of extraordinary mishaps. We had to assemble at Columbus Circle at 7 a.m. for the entire package show to board two Greyhound buses. There were two bands from England in a line-up that included singer Anita O'Day, the Lennie Tristano Quintet, the Thelonious Monk Quartet and George Shearing's Big Band with the Adderley brothers as guest soloists. In charge of the tour was a mild-mannered, bespectacled man called Arnold London, an accountant by profession who had taken on the tour as a favour to the promoter. He lived to rue the day he opened his big mouth. At the outset his nerves were palpably far from robust. The first time we stopped at a roadhouse for a snack, I noticed that as soon as he was perched on a stool he tipped several different-coloured pills and capsules on to the counter and swallowed them at strategic moments before, during and after the light meal.

Arnie's troubles began right there at Columbus Circle. The English contingent arrived slightly before seven, to avoid the catastrophe of being late and seeing the coaches glide sleekly away dead on time. One by one the rest of the cast assembled so that by 9 a.m. almost everyone was there. Everyone but Thelonious Monk. Monk, a founding father of Modern Jazz, has a well-publicised reputation as an eccentric, so we had hardly expected to see him bustle up on the stroke of seven, but by ten o'clock it had become apparent that he wasn't going to arrive at all of his own volition. After some agitated phoning, Arnie herded us on board and we made a trip into the suburbs to pick him up. We pulled out of New York at 11 a.m. bound for Columbus, Ohio.

Honourable mention should be made here of Thelonious Monk's hat. It plays a leading part in this story because, according to Arnold London's astonished report, Monk was sitting up in bed wearing it when a deputation from the road management called upon him with an invitation to join us all on the bus. The hat had been given to him by an admirer. It was a sort of wickerwork lampshade, or inverted fruit basket, probably Chinese in origin, with long straps which dangled over the ears. We got to know that hat well since at no time in the day (or, presumably, night) did Monk remove it. For ten days it was a fixture. Then on the eleventh day, boarding the coach in Boston, Massachussetts, Monk appeared in a different hat. It was a grey, bulbous affair which mystified us until we recognised it as a Homburg in the state in which it was stored on the

126

hatter's shelf, before a gentle karate chop had given it the conventional dent in the top. 'Hey, Monk, you've changed your hat!' someone cried in amazement. 'Sure,' said Monk without a flicker, 'you can't wear the same hat all the time.'

I suppose I am not the one to talk when it comes to hats. I used to be quite a collector of head-gear at one time and colleagues would bring back specimens for me from their travels. In America I was wearing a Spanish flamenco hat, one of those jaunty black affairs with flat top and wide brim. After consistent wear it had a dusty, crumpled look which led Monk, I learned later, to believe that he had seen his first genuine Western-style cowboy. He was bitterly disappointed to learn that I was British.

It was on the bus on the way to Columbus that it was discovered that Anita O'Day had no accompanist for the tour. She had relied upon enrolling one of the pianists in the package, but all the pianists bar one were bandleaders with their own star spots on the bill. The exception was my pianist, Ian Armit, who was leaned on heavily by a distraught management to step in and assist her. For Ian, the acute first-night nerves which we were all suffering were augmented by the task of learning Anita's arrangements at a few moments' notice. Before the show she agreed to simplify her breakneck version of 'Tea for Two', full of complex bits of arrangement, so as not to make things too hard for him. When he went on stage at the start of her spot, he found that the stage lighting didn't allow him to see the music. He struggled through the early songs pretty well, but when it came to 'Tea for Two', Miss O'Day either forgot or ignored the pre-arranged plan and reverted to a routine which he didn't know. To make matters worse, she signalled to him to take a piano solo at the hair-raising tempo. Sitting out front, the rest of our band watched with sinking hearts, and were immensely cheered when, in mid-solo, he stopped playing and shattered the awesome atmosphere with a stentorian Scottish

You can't wear
the same
hat all the
time...

Thelonious
Monk

cry of 'Oh, shit ! ! ! ' Afterwards, Anita O'Day took the episode with remarkably bad grace, complaining to everyone she met backstage, 'Did you see what they did to me? They gave me a *Dixieland* piano-player!' We became fair friends with Anita on the tour—friendly enough to remind her that nobody had *given* her a piano-player. She'd commandeered one and had no right to complain.

Our driver on the tour, in the second of the two Greyhound buses, was an expatriate Irishman called Eugene Quinn, who looked like a youthful Edmund O'Brien. His colleague in the front bus was a toughie with white hair who showed neither dismay nor remorse when he missed a turning off the freeway en route for Cleveland and took us 137 miles out of our way. When the mistake was discovered, our cortège of two buses pulled off into a service area and for a while we ate ice-cream in leisurely fashion, mulling over with a sort of ruminative complacency the thought that we would probably miss the concert. In the end we reached Cleveland just in time for the openers on the show to go straight on stage in their travelling clothes while the rest changed frantically in the hotel, which was luckily right across from the theatre. Eugene never really recovered from this. His driving for the rest of the tour had a panic-stricken air and the cry of 'Take it easy, Gene!' emanating from all parts of the coach, including sometimes the lavatory at the back, became a recurring theme.

I missed the next disaster, a journey from Boston to New York in which the coaches couldn't find their way on to the motorway and fumbled through the night and long into the morning along minor roads. I had meanwhile been sent ahead by plane to make a promotional television appearance. On the plane, a stewardess, after peering at me long and hard every time she passed, eventually came up and said, with great charm, 'Pardon my intrusion, but are you by any chance related to Claude Raines?' As a boy I had been movie-crazy and was well-acquainted with the sardonic face of Claude Raines, whom I took to be no more than about five-foot three and knocking on a bit even in those days. So I made a rather surprised denial. 'Gee, that's funny,' she said. 'You look so like him I thought you must be his brother.'

The hectic rush to the airport, the solitary journey and the mistaken identification with one of Hollywood's more venerable citizens put me generally in a disgruntled mood and it is my cherished belief that I out-nastied Henry Morgan, a TV anchor-man of, apparently, great popularity in the States at that time, whose stock-in-trade was a studied, smirking offensiveness to everyone in range. They put me at ease just before the show by telling me that he had crucified Andy Williams the week before. When I went on he tried to needle me by asking, in a tone of amused surprise, what an Englishman was doing playing jazz in America. Just the same, I said, as Americans are doing speaking English in England. After that the interview rambled along fairly tamely and quite soon, Henry moved on to the next item, which so far as I recall was an abortive phone-call to Mr. Kruschev, then on a state visit in Washington, to ask him what he had for supper.

The evening concert at the New York Town Hall was a nerve-racking occasion. For one thing, the Town Hall is almost as hallowed in jazz history as the Carnegie Hall itself. It was from there that Eddie Condon's famous jam-sessions of the mid-'forties were broadcast to England, and it was there, too, that Louis Armstrong made a significant and historic appearance in 1947, playing after years of big-band work with a small improvising outfit which paved the way for his subsequent All Stars. What made the event even more awesome for me was that our show's compère, Willis Connover, familiar the world over as the voice on the Voice of America Jazz Hour, had left the package and the management decided that I should introduce the show. News came backstage that Benny Goodman was in the audience, not to mention several of the heavy guns among the New York critical fraternity, men with resounding names like Whitney Balliett and John S. Wilson. Fortunately, the band was in especially good fettle on the night and bagged most of the good reviews. As for the compèring, I recall little other than one tentative joke which fell flat on its face. That morning in the hotel I had watched a TV quiz-show in which a woman contestant had been denied a $3,000 prize for saying that the River Clyde was in the British Isles. 'I'm sorry,' said the quizmaster, oozing condolence, 'the answer should have been Scotland.' I told the story as it stands and one man, a Scot no doubt, guffawed somewhere in the balcony. I like to think that perhaps Benny Goodman smiled. He is, after all, a much-travelled man.

The New York Town Hall Concert ended in a shambles. George Shearing's Big Band used to finish the show, with Julian 'Cannonball' Adderley and his brother Nat making their guest appearance in the first set. The stage-manager at the Town Hall was it seems, a Jobsworth ('it's as much as my job's worth') of a kind thought to thrive only in Britain. Over here we're used to recalcitrant officials with unbending ways. (My whole band was once refused re-admission to a theatre in Blackpool after a visit to the nearest pub in the interval, even though we were due onstage at the start of the second half. 'I *know* who you are,' the old walrus at the stage-door reiterated, 'but my strict orders are "no readmission during the concert!"' It's as much as my job's worth . . .') We didn't expect to find similar obstructiveness in the Land of Opportunity. But on the stroke of ten-thirty, when our concert was due to finish, the stage-manager of the New York Town Hall dropped the curtain. To make matters worse, he dropped it on top of George Shearing, who had stepped forward from the piano to announce the Adderley brothers. George, who is of course blind, must have thought that the skies had fallen in on him. Despite pleas from the concert promoters, the man refused to allow the concert to go on a minute longer, and the night ended in a babel of recriminations and abuse.

The upshot was that George Shearing, who I think had had about enough of the rigours of this particular tour, pulled his whole band off the show. We set off for Pittsburgh next morning without them—and without Thelonious Monk, too, who had decided to charter a plane so that he could stay a little longer in New York. We were still without them when the concert started—ironically, the first and only total sell-out of the tour. Frantic negotiations had failed to pacify George Shearing in time for him to make the show, and, we learned later, Thelonious Monk was at Pittsburgh Airport in time, but for some reason wasn't allowed to disembark. So in place of the usual climax to the concert, a jam-session was hastily assembled from volunteers from the cast.

That the version we played of 'All the Things You Are' lasted interminably was no fault of mine. Lennie Tristano, who was at the piano, has always been one of the most advanced musical theorists in jazz. (He also proved a smart tactician at cards. Being blind, he made certain that his sighted opponents gained no advantage. One of my band, going to the coach at night to fetch something, tripped over the Lennie Tristano Quintet. They were playing poker in the pitch dark with Braille cards.) Lennie's colleagues, saxophonists Lee Konitz and Warne Marsh, had come up in the same experimental musical school. Britishers like Jimmy Skidmore and Ronnie Ross could keep up with them. I couldn't, so I stood on stage holding my trumpet, admiring the ingenious complexities of their improvisations and watching the audience, many of whom had come to hear George Shearing, stream out in their hundreds.

The most lasting friendship we made on the tour was with Charlie Rouse, the tenor-saxist with the Thelonious Monk Quartet. Through him I managed to pierce at least the outer layer of the enigmatic armour in which Thelonious has encased

132

himself. Monk belongs to a long line of jazz nonconformists, musicians who have achieved original self-expression by hacking out a difficult and uncharted route of their own. Standing in the wings listening to Monk night after night, watching him wander off around the stage while Charlie Rouse was soloing and occasionally execute a little lumbering dance for his own private amusement, I acquired a strong affection for that prodding, unseductive piano style which, according to Charlie, constantly sent out startling messages to his musicians to keep them on their metal. Jabbing away at the keyboard, sometimes appearing to hit two notes at once by accident and then to return to them to repeat the effect, Monk always seemed to me to play the piano like a man who had only that day discovered the instrument for the first time. As a man I never got close to him, although we did achieve a strange sort of reticent rapport. 'Humphrey, I got you covered,' he said when we were making our farewells. It was the verbal equivalent of a wink and a thumbs-up, and said everything.

On his subsequent visits to England I saw him and the Quartet whenever possible, once going out to Heathrow to meet him. On that occasion, the airport press photographer tried to set up a photograph with Monk and myself. He wanted a conventional jolly picture and asked me to fling my arms around Monk in a gesture of welcome. It was not a gesture that came naturally to either of us, so the photographer tried a solo shot instead. 'Raise your cap, Mr. Monk,' he kept saying, 'Look as if you're saying "Hello, England!"' Monk was wearing a conventional flat cap on this occasion and, with a sleepy expression of compliance, he raised it—but from behind! There were no pictures of Monk's arrival in the evening papers that night.

When I flew back from America after just three weeks in the place, I was bursting with get-up-and-go. Life in little ol' England wuz—sorry, was—going to be different from now on! For

133

about two weeks astonished friends and colleagues were subjected to merciless hustling, accompanied by impatient snapping of the fingers to signify that I expected things to move—where to, I didn't care, so long as they got up and went! It didn't last long. Quite soon I had settled back into the familiar pace at which I have been content to cruise along ever since.

Condon

EDDIE CONDON was a very funny man. He was also, on his own ready admission, a boozer. Perhaps his greatest claim to distinction, apart from the devoted and tireless work which he put to the cause of jazz over the whole of his lifetime, was the ability to be drunk and funny at the same time. Indeed, in the short time that I knew him, when my band toured Britain with his in the 'fifties, I never really discovered whether he could be sober and funny.

The advance publicity for his tour was almost exclusively alcoholic, and his arrival personified it. A team of British musicians, myself included, went out to the airport to meet him. With us was singer Beryl Bryden, a big girl in heart and personality as well as in frame, and a boundless enthusiast for jazz wherever it is played in the world. Beryl had brought her washboard along to supplement the rhythm section. Eddie Condon and drummer George Wettling emerged together from the airport building, having manifestly spent the journey from New York drowning their mutual dislike of air-travel. The first thing that Eddie saw, in a Britain which was totally new to him, was a large lady thrashing a washboard. It stopped him in his tracks and for a few minutes he and George had to lean against each other for support. In the general

135

hubbub of greetings he recovered himself and was next seen disappearing head-first into the pitch-black baggage compartment of an airport bus, mumbling, 'There must be a bed in here somewhere!'

At the Cumberland Hotel, a crowd of musicians and reporters assembled in Eddie Condon's room. A huge tray of multiple Scotches was sent up and an informal Press conference began, with the principal subject of it lying in a crumpled heap face-down on the bed. For a while the questions of the gentlemen of the Press were answered from the muffled depths of a pillow, until one rather needled young man from the *Daily Express* asked with some acidity if Mr. Condon could possibly sit up. 'Sure' said Mr. Condon, turning the right way round with some difficulty, '. . . but you know, I'm no athlete.'

Later the same day, Eddie, having abandoned all hope of recuperative sleep, was hustled off to Lime Grove to take part in an interview with Geoffrey Johnson-Smith in the BBC 'Tonight' programme. The resulting chat, captured on scores of amateur tape-recordings, has long been a collector's piece among connoisseurs of the surrealistic. At one point Eddie floored his interviewer by dredging up from somewhere in his fuddled subconscious a word that can't have been in general usage since Doctor Johnson's day. 'Look,' he said, 'I don't want to veridicalise any pronouns . . .' Later, when Eddie explained that his hands were too small for piano-playing, Geoffrey Johnson-Smith said, rather weakly, 'So that's why you stick to the guitar.' Eddie affected a startled look. 'Do I stick to my guitar?' At the end, a relieved Johnson-Smith said, 'I'm not sure that I've been with you all the way, but thank you.'

After the BBC interview there was a formal Press conference and jam-session at a London restaurant. Cornetist Wild Bill Davison, whose hobby of antique-collecting afforded Eddie much scope for sardonic wit, was late arriving. 'Where is Mr. Davison?' somebody asked. 'I don't know,' barked Eddie. 'He's

136

probably out unscrewing Big Ben.'

We travelled for most of our three week tour in a coach, each man with a personal bottle of Scotch, renewed at the start of each day and reinforced with bottled beer from crates stashed in every available nook. As we ate—or rather drank—up the miles, it was interesting to compare the musicians' reaction to what was almost non-stop re-fuelling. The trombonist Cutty Cuttshall, a big, quiet-mannered man of Red Indian descent with one of the most impressive abdomens ever seen since man began to walk upright, would sit quietly most of the day until the alcohol reached a critical level, at which point he would let out a fearsome Indian war-whoop to let everyone know that, whatever action might transpire, he was ready for it. George Wettling, one of the great drummers in jazz, would gradually turn from a sociable and humorous Dr. Jekyll into an argumentative and 'salty' Mr. Hyde, finding particular provocation in the unruffled back view of Wild Bill Davison's head a few seats in front of him. His theme in this mood was usually that, without his guiding and goading beat behind them, none of the other musicians could really play at all. 'You hear them high notes he plays,' he would wheeze, jabbing a finger in the direction of Wild Bill, 'he doesn't play them, *I do*!!' This crescendo of disaffection usually reached the same climax. George would get out into the aisle, ready, it seemed, to take on anyone. He would find his way blocked by the full frontal authority of Cutty Cuttshall, looming over him, his big-checked lumberjack shirt bulging threateningly. The confrontation was rather a sweet one. 'George,' Cutty would say quite quietly, 'be nice!' And George, with no physique to match the red-checked protuberance that barred his way, would sit down.

Cutty and George are both dead now but Wild Bill Davison looked, when I met him again in 1975, barely a day older, confirming my belief that he knew well how to look after himself. There were times on that tour when, to my certain knowledge, he didn't see the inside of his hotel room until 7 am. At 9 am. he would emerge for the coach call looking as carefully groomed and bustlingly alert as a businessman going to a high-level meeting and, as always, chewing purposefully. (Eddie Condon once wrote, 'Nobody has ever found out what Davison does with his gum while playing, but he must have some special cavity for it—something similar to a kangaroo pouch.') Once on the coach, others slept, drank, and otherwise recuperated. Bill talked, from Land's End to John o' Groats. Richard Gehman, Eddie Condon's literary collaborator, tells a story that is characteristic of both Bill and Eddie. At one time, Wild Bill 'took to making lamps out of old horns. He was obsessed with this hobby for a long time—at least three days—and could talk of nothing else. One night while on the stand at Condon's Club, Bill was chattering away to Cutty Cuttshall about his lamp-making project while Eddie was vainly attempting to beat off the band. Eddie finally grew exasperated. "Listen, you son of a bitch," he said to Davison, "will you quit that gabbin', pick up that lamp and play it?"'

Eddie Condon didn't always travel with us on the coach. When he did, he rarely had more than one eye open, with which he surveyed the passing British countryside with profound disbelief. Once we stopped at a West Country pub and straggled into the public bar for a lunch break. Along the walls, rheumy-eyed locals surveyed us silently. Eddie Condon, furnished with a large Scotch, went over to fraternise. For a minute or so he stood, hat rakishly on the back of his head, and matched their stares. Then he rapped out an opening gambit. 'Are you guys poachers?'

In places where the legend of Eddie Condon and the Chicago era had barely penetrated, audiences were bewildered and sometimes antagonised by Eddie's casual presentation and disinclination to push himself as anything more than the organiser of the band. 'Why don't you play a guitar solo?'

138

taunted someone at a Bristol concert. 'Because I can't!' retorted Eddie with cheerful candour. As compère of the whole show I felt called on to act as a sort of interpreter of the Condon message, which was, in effect, 'I've got these good musicians together—now listen to them and don't worry about me.' It wasn't always easy. On one show he arrived late, his manager having had difficulty prising him out of an afternoon nap. His band played several numbers without him. To cover up, I went on stage as soon as he was ready and announced blandly, '. . .And now, the star of our show, Eddie Condon!!' It was my bad luck that the star of our show, so far from appearing in suitably imposing style, weaved on somewhat diffidently having forgotten to put on his bow tie.

I also had trouble getting Eddie to do encores. By the end of each concert, when my band joined Eddie's in a final jam-session, all earlier derelictions were forgotten and the audience went wild, clamouring for more. Eddie would mutter in my ear, 'Let's get out of here', I would say 'I think perhaps one more number. . .', Eddie would cock his bad ear (he was partially deaf in one ear) in my direction and say, 'I didn't hear you say anything.'

As Sidney Bechet once noted—and he didn't usually lavish praise on those on the entrepreneural side of the fence—Eddie did more for jazz than most, worked hard for it all his life, played it on his four-string guitar better than anyone imagined and remained, withal, 'a nice little guy'.

Bechet

SIDNEY BECHET had curious links with Britain over the years. A travelling man for most of his life, he was one of the first jazz musicians to come here, as long ago as 1919. His early impression of England underwent a traumatic metamorphosis. He was then with Will Marion Cook's Southern Syncopated Orchestra, and, during its season at the Philharmonic Hall in London, the band was commanded to send a small contingent along to play at Buckingham Palace for King George V, who has been noted earlier as being quite a jazzer in his own quiet way.

Bechet doesn't seem to have been overawed by the interior of the Palace—'it was like Grand Central Station with a lot of carpets and things on the walls'. What impressed him most was the sight of the monarch, in the flesh and large as life—or small as life, if we are to be strictly accurate. In his autobiography *Treat it Gentle* Bechet wrote, 'It was the first time I ever got to recognise someone from having seen his picture on my money . . . it was a funny thing, looking at your money and seeing someone you know!'

It was only a matter of months before he was to hurl all that money overboard into the Atlantic as a gesture of disgust for all things British. As a result of a bedroom fracas with a

141

Sidney Bechet recognises his money..

prostitute—his account of it suggests a sort of escalating slap and tickle which ended with the lady screaming murder and rape out of the window—he was arrested. Although he was cleared of attempted rape and assault and battery, he was ordered to be deported as an 'undesirable alien'. It was on the way home that he decided to sever relations by flinging the assorted likenesses of George V into the sea.

Returning exactly thirty years later, Sidney still found the occasion nerve-wracking. Mind you, there was more than just the hangover of that court case to worry about. In 1949 the reciprocal embargo between the British and American Musicians' Unions was still in force. Some British promoters decided to defy it, and Bechet and Coleman Hawkins were each brought in as 'tourists' with the specific aim of featuring them on separate concerts. In the face of the combined opposition of the Musicians' Union and the Ministry of Labour, the ruse by which Bechet was presented to the public was a naïve one. My band was booked to give a concert at the Wintergardens Theatre in London. In the middle of the concert, surprise, surprise, Sidney Bechet was picked out by a spotlight in a box near the stage, and was prevailed upon by the compére and audience together to join us on stage for a few numbers. Two days later I made a feeble attempt to persuade a Scotland Yard inspector who called at my house that the two-hour rehearsal which we had gone through with Sidney in the afternoon was not a rehearsal at all but a social gathering at which, quite by chance, some music was played. The promoters were summoned and fined £100 for employing aliens without a work permit. I suppose I was lucky not to be had up as an accessory before, during and after the event. Of course there was no question of bribery and corruption, but I do recall that, having taken down my statement in laborious longhand and obtained my signature to it, the inspector asked for my autograph on behalf of his daughter, who was a fan.

143

By the time the case came up, Bechet was back home in America, no doubt happy to have escaped more legal trouble but satisfied that the 'rape' incident of thirty years earlier had been expunged from the bureaucratic memory. The concert had been a great triumph for him. A new-found interest in the sound and history of New Orleans jazz was then at its height in Britain, and when Sidney was introduced and walked on stage playing his soprano saxophone, the great roar from the audience completely drowned the music.

At that meeting and at a recording session which we did on the previous day, we got on well with Bechet who, in turn, was in a mellow mood. It wasn't always so. Wally Fawkes, then with me on clarinet, left the band in the early Fifties on a four-week sabbatical to play in a European band assembled by Bechet in Geneva. He told us on his return of a first rehearsal at which the maestro, suddenly flying into a violent rage, castigated the eager young Europeans so ferociously that their insides turned to water. Afterwards Wally, not a man to be long overawed, asked him if the band had really been as bad as he had said. 'Oh, the band's fine,' said Sidney, 'I just did that to be sure you'd work hard!'

By this time, Bechet had taken up permanent residence in Paris. His early experiences in France were as unpromising as those in Britain. In 1929, during a row in the street with some other expatriate American musicians, Bechet drew a gun and pumped bullets in all directions, one of which found its final resting-place in the flesh of a French woman who was watching the extraordinary Wild West scene at what she thought was a safe distance. For this outburst, Bechet was sent to prison for eleven months. The story was once rife in the jazz magazines that it was this experience that turned his hair prematurely white, a theory which is modified, if not discounted altogether, by subsequent photographs in the Forties showing a greying but not snowy head. Anyway, it was clear when Bechet returned to post-war France, first as a visitor and later to live, that, as in Britain, all was forgotten and forgiven.

It's a common and understandable wish among jazz fans through the ages that their idols should be lovable. Many of the people who were able to meet Bechet often after he came to Europe, and who experienced his courteous, soft-spoken and considerate manner on social occasions, speak of him still in terms of cuddly affection. My experience is that jazzmen, particularly those who have fought their way almost single-handed to the top of their profession, are as cuddly as man-eating tigers. Bechet wrote of himself, 'I can be mean. It takes an awful lot: someone's got to do a lot to me. But when I do get mean, I can be powerful mean.' In its American sense, 'mean' covers many shades of temperament from evil temper to mere cussedness. It was these lower reaches of meanness which I saw most often in Bechet—and found, as someone never at any time on the receiving end, strongly endearing. I like my heroes to be men of iron, not of cotton-wool and fur. Indeed, it would have astounded and appalled me to discover that music of such passion, command, ferocity and seductiveness had emanated from a Teddy Bear.

Once Bechet was established in France, he became a national hero. His wedding in 1951, to a German lady, was in his own words 'one of the biggest things that's ever been seen since Aly Khan's marriage'. Held in Antibes, it took the form of a New Orleans Mardi Gras parade, with bride and bridegroom in an open landau followed by a retinue of bands. It helped to establish Sidney in France as a superstar in the Chevalier/Piaf category. Two or three years after his state wedding I visited him in Paris, in a second home which he had established across the other side of the city with a second 'wife', a girl of seventeen, by whom he had then a small son. I was told that he commuted, allegedly 'on tour', between these two households. When I called on him unexpectedly at this second

145

home, our conversation was punctuated by the scolding of his young mistress who had discovered a third liaison with a girl in Lausanne.

That Bechet had not lost his sexual attractiveness at an age estimated at somewhere between fifty-five and sixty became apparent from an episode in the now defunct Queens Hotel in Birmingham during his 1956 tour here. A lady knocked on the door of his room at a late hour, saying that she had been a fan of his for many years and would like a talk with him. 'Take off your clothes and we'll talk,' was Bechet's unsubtle reply. Next morning he picked up the phone in his single room and ordered breakfast for two.

On that tour, Bechet was the guest soloist with a French band led by Andre Reweliotty, and my own band toured with them, opening the show for an hour and coming back on for the finale. There is a saying that an Alsatian dog is perfectly safe and harmless unless you show it that you are frightened, at which point it is liable to take your arm off at the elbow. The same, in that late stage in his life, can be said of Sidney Bechet. The French musicians, with one notable exception, were scared stiff of him and he tyranised them unmercifully. By this time he had acquired a secretary-cum-road manager in the shape of Claude Wolff, who later married Petula Clark. Through him he imposed strict rules on the band. After a concert they were to return to the hotel with him and, after a meal or a snack, retire to bed when he did. With Reweliotty's band on this tour was a highly-strung and excitable pianist called Eddie Bernard, whom I had met some years early at a jazz festival in France and who was only deputising temporarily with the French band. The diminutive Eddie rebelled from the start against the rules laid down by Bechet, and it was clear that there was going to be trouble.

Trouble came when we hit Glasgow, where no jazz concert took place without an all-night party afterwards at the home of

Norman McSwan, jazz enthusiast, record-collector, amateur discographer and, in such time as remained, distinguished heart surgeon. As on previous occasions, Eddie Bernard was resolved to defy the Bechet edict and come out with us to the party. He might have got away with it had he not decided, on checking in at the Central Hotel, to change his room before leaving for the concert on the grounds that it overlooked the street and would be too noisy. Claude Wolff had a list of the rooms so that he could call the band for an early start next morning. Eddie forgot to give him his new room-number. The Central Hotel has 270 rooms, and when Eddie predictably overslept next morning after a party that ended at 7 am, a combined posse of Claude Wolff, Sidney Bechet and the entire French band had to knock on 200 of them before they found him.

On the train heading for the next gig, my band and I watched the sequel in gleeful fascination. At one end of the open compartment a sort of kangaroo court assembled around Bechet, the Frenchmen wearing expressions of addled solemnity and Sidney sitting in the corner looking like an oriental overlord about to order an execution. Eddie was then summoned and, despite a spirited and cheerfully insubordinate defence, was told that he would thenceforward return to his hotel immediately after each concert and attend no further parties.

Two or three days later there was another all-night shindig in Liverpool at the home of one of the members of the Merseyssippi Jazz Band. We told Eddie that it was not to be missed at any cost, and arranged to smuggle him out of the theatre after the concert and take him there. Unfortunately the Frenchmen got wind of the plan and, under Bechet's maliciously-satisfied eye, took him from us and hauled him on board the coach and away. Over a Chinese meal, we and the musicians from the Merseyssippi Band hatched a plot to kidnap him. A marauding posse was sent to the Adelphi hotel, where they caught Bechet's party just as it was trooping off to bed. Literally from under Bechet's nose, Eddie Bernard was seized and whisked into a waiting car which roared away into the suburbs for the party. When I saw Sidney next morning, there was an evil but by no means hostile glint in his eye. 'I hear Eddie Bernard enjoyed the party last night,' he said meaningfully. I agreed, and after a pause he said, 'I was tired last night, but if I hadn't been, I'd have come right out after him!'

Louis

WHEN INTERVIEWERS ASK, 'Did you know Louis Armstrong?', I have no idea what to say. I saw him often, spent quite a lot of time in his company and was, I think, looked upon by him as one of a handful of close friends in Britain. But I doubt if anyone knew him. To friend and foe alike there was, deep below the surface of companionship and bonhomie, an inpenetrable wall in which every stone was an enigma. Did the genius who endowed jazz with new dimensions in musical range and emotional depth really aspire no higher than the chocolate-box sentimentality of Guy Lombardo, his favourite band? Were slogans like 'You gotta stay in front of the public' and 'All I want to do is just keep hittin' those notes' truly at the root of his creative philosophy? What made a man who clearly cared nothing for wealth and possessions (he was forty-two before he bought his first modest home, and he died in it twenty-nine years later) pursue commercial success with such rigorous single-mindedness? And how does one reconcile a ruthless success story with the love, warmth and sheer happiness which were generously dispensed by its central character and which were returned to him with interest by all who heard him? No one will ever have a confident answer to these and other equally intransigent questions. One can only guess.

I was jolted into a spasm of conjecture by a startlingly un-characteristic comment which Louis let slip during one of his visits in the middle 'sixties. He was on his way back to the States after a crippling tour of one-night stands across the world, and I went out to Heathrow in the early morning to see him off. We were perched on stools having breakfast in the restaurant. Louis' face was creased with fatigue. He talked wistfully about a year's vacation 'doin' nothin'—a little fishin', maybe, and goin' around listenin' to some of the cats blowin'.' Then, after a pause, he added wearily, 'Yes, show business is a drag!'

In the light of Louis Armstrong's patent professionalism, the frequently expressed dedication to his trumpet and to the enter-tainer's life, it was as if Bobby Charlton had been overheard asking 'Who needs football?' or the Archbishop of Canterbury caught jumping up and down on his vestments.

'Show business is a drag!' may well have been a momentary expression of dissatisfaction. But it was a significant early sign of impatience with the whole rigmarole of show-business and the laugh-and-the-world-laughs-with-you conventions. When Louis arrived at London Airport in 1968 for a two-week season at the Batley Variety Club, he was in one of the monu-mental rages which have stood out like startling monoliths on the otherwise smooth plainlands of a remarkably equable tem-perament. The band had been travelling for many hours with-out sleep, an American fellow-passenger had been needling Louis on the plane and in the arrival lounge, and a row had broken out among the musicians themselves. I learned the details later, but when I heard him speaking to an interviewer on the BBC radio 'Today' programme that morning, it was clear that Louis was not his usual mellow, paternal self. The young reporter unconsciously adopted a hectoring line, going so far at one stage as to question Armstrong's encouraging remarks about a young schoolboy trumpet-player who had greeted him at the airport. 'Well, I suppose as a celebrity you

150

have to say that!' This questioning of his sincerity in circumstances in which generosity and encouragement came as naturally to him as breathing clearly deeply offended Louis and thenceforward he answered questions in a loud, strained voice and in unusually aggressive style, at one point seemingly condemning the whole pestilential race of spot-interviewers with the phrase 'The trouble with *you* guys is. . .'

When he returned to Britain in 1970 for a charity concert headed by David Frost on behalf of the Playing Fields Association, it was once again apparent that the veneer of showbiz bonhomie had, in advanced age, worn thin. To the normal stresses of answering repetitive and not always well-researched questions was now added the matter of his age. His seventieth birthday had come and gone, and like Duke Ellington a year before him, he was subjected to a line of enquiry which seemed to presuppose that for an entertainer in the jazz field to reach the allotted span of three score years and ten was an unusual occurrence verging on the miraculous. In the previous year, musicians taking part in a David Frost TV programme were startled—and, it must be said, gleeful—when at rehearsal a sound link-up with Duke Ellington's dressing-room in a London theatre caught the usually urbane and suave maestro in a towering passion, calling upon some unseen minion to 'get these m-f's off my back!' The m-f's had apparently mentioned his age once too often. Louis Armstrong's reaction to the heavily tactless harping upon age and retirement was more specific. A perspiring Alan Hargreaves, interviewing him for the Thames Television 'Today' programme, ran unwittingly into a fierce counter-attack when he broached the subject. 'It seems like you people *want* me to retire!' was Louis's aggrieved response, followed by a more spirited and characteristic outburst. 'What d'you expect me to do—go back on that cart sellin' coal with that ol' mule fartin' in my face?' Happily this momentary break in rapport was, according to Alan Hargreaves, patched up in Louis' hotel-room afterwards, when Louis went out of his way to put Alan at his ease.

Being as romantically-inclined as the next jazz fan, I nursed, for a few weeks after the 'show-business is a drag' incident, the belief that the villain of the piece was Joe Glaser, the powerful head of the massive Associated Booking Corporation, into whose care and protection Louis had delivered himself in 1935 when Joe was just starting up in the agency business. It was easy to type-cast Joe Glaser as the 'baddy'. I first met him at a jazz festival in France in 1948. I was sitting alone in a box at the theatre listening to Louis Armstrong's All Stars when Glaser came in and stood behind me. Sensing his grey presence—he had the steely but at the same time lugubrious look of a supporting player in an Edward G. Robinson movie—I felt I should say something. 'Fantastic!' I breathed, gesturing towards the six Olympians on stage. 'Maybe,' was his deflating response, 'but if I wanna know if it's good, I look down there', and he jabbed a thumb in the direction of the audience. Clearly my own playing at the festival, about which Louis made some encouraging noises, didn't fulfil Joe's audience-orientated criteria. When a British entrepeneur suggested a few years later that Glaser might handle an American tour by me and my band, Joe's answer was short and to the point. 'Lyttelton? Schmyttelton.'

So I was quite ready to put Louis' apparent enslavement in the showbiz treadmill down to exploitation by Glaser. Someone more reckless than I did once put this suggestion to Joe himself, and he was genuinely outraged. '*You* get him to stop playing' he cried. It was at this point that, doing research for a now-abandoned book on Louis, I dug up at any rate one feasible answer to the Armstrong riddle. The keynote of his career was something far more basic than either Art or Money. It was Survival.

152

Medium-sized H.L., slim Joe Temperley, and Big Joe Turner

Mr Five-by-Five: 'Little' Jimmy Rushing

Wrestler's trick, one-handed: Buck Clayton with H.L.

British Buck

Thelonius Monk: 'Hello, England!'

Sidney Bechet and H.L.

To encore or not to encore: Eddie Condon and H.L. (*photo T. Cryer*)

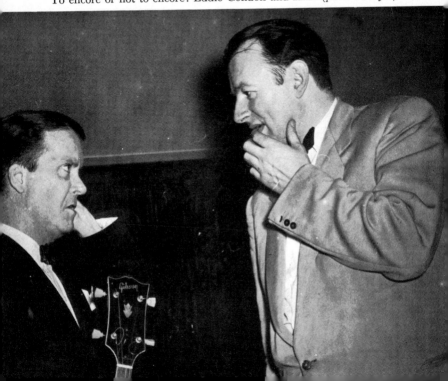

Louis listening to H.L.'s band at 100 Oxford Street, 1956

The character of the itinerant jazz musician in general and Louis Armstrong in particular has a certain Wild West flavour about it. Have trumpet, will travel. From the moment when, as a boy in New Orleans, he turned away from incipient delinquency towards a career in music, his life was spent with a trumpet in his hand. Subsidiary talents—as singer, entertainer, movie actor—manifested themselves later, but Louis and the trumpet were indivisible.

He looked after both with care bordering on hypochondria. Once, on arrival at London Airport, he borrowed a trumpet from Spike MacIntosh (himself a fine performer and Armstrong devotee), his own instrument having been whisked away with the band's baggage. When Louis had ripped off a few characteristic phrases for the cameramen, he returned the instrument to Spike, who asked eagerly how it had played. 'That's a good horn,' said Louis 'but you need to put some of that hot water through it . . . get rid of all them newts and saveloys!'

Louis Armstrong's attentiveness to his own plumbing had become legendary by the end of his life. After his charity appearance for the Playing Fields Association, he was given a small token gift by the Duke of Edinburgh at a special presentation to mark the occasion. Louis gave the Duke in return a pocket of Swiss Kriss, explaining its purpose and function in a forthright and sibilant monosyllable. Beneath the lavatorial comedy of Louis' association with Swiss Kriss lay serious crusading zeal. I once engaged in lengthy correspondence with an ardent Irish friend of Armstrong's, Maxwell Norris. Max knew Louis well when he came to London in the early thirties, always referred to him as 'my guru' and saw him as a forefather, in many respects, of the Love Generation of the Sixties. In those days, Louis had adopted marihuana in preference to alcohol and had clearly studied the teachings of Gaylord Hauser, from which the herbal laxative Swiss Kriss emanated. For the rest of

153

his life he combated a gargantuan appetite with sporadic diet-ing, so that the jazz photo-albums show a startling alternation between a plump and slender Satchmo. His verdict on Bunny Berigan—'a fine trumpet-man but he had no business dying that young'—was a simple statement of his belief, and there can be few trumpet-players on the face of the globe who did not come away from a visit to Louis regaled with a type-written diet-sheet, several small tins of 'Louis Armstrong Lip Salve' and enough Swiss Kriss to evacuate an army.

The stuff is certainly effective. The late Duggie Tobutt, road-manager to the Harold Davison Office and a man beloved of every visiting American jazz-musician, once succumbed to Louis' insistence and took the prescribed dessertspoonful of Swiss Kriss last thing before retiring. At noon the following day, the telephone rang in Louis' hotel room. It was Duggie, ringing to enquire, in a voice which he dared not project above a whisper, if there was 'any antidote to this stuff'.

When Louis Armstrong's All Stars came to London in 1956 and my band shared the bill with them for ten days at the Empress Hall, I noticed that, for a period before the first con-cert and between shows, visitors would be ushered away from his dressing-room and even his wife Lucille would withdraw. It wasn't until the band left London on tour and I travelled out to see them in Manchester that I discovered what ritual took place behind that closed and closely-guarded door. The backstage area at Bellevue was deserted during the two shows, and Louis' valet Doc Pugh, reporting to Louis that I was there, was sent to summon me to the dressing-room. Louis was relaxing between shows, stark naked except for a handkerchief bound round his head to keep his hair in place, and a complex jock-strap. I quickly sensed that my presence alone was enough for him—he rarely called upon his friends to say or do anything, but simply to *be* there. Conversation anyway was ruled out, because while I sat and watched he massaged creamy lip-salve into the famous

154

embattled 'chops' and then covered them, top and bottom, with gauze. I believe he did say something when the dressing was completed, but that well-known astrakhan voice, vibrating loosely in relaxation and emerging from a thick sandwich of gauze, conveyed no more than a cavernous growl of greeting.

Of course, giving attention to the serious business—in Louis' mind, even duty—of staying alive and in good working order, was a means to survival. So, too, was the perfecting and burnishing of his trumpet technique. He was not, strictly speaking, a self-taught musician. The rudiments of the instrument were taught to him in the Waifs' Home in New Orleans to which he was sent for a year or two in his early 'teens, and subsequently he had to master sight-reading to cope with work in big organised bands like Fletcher Henderson's Orchestra and Erskine Tate's Theatre Orchestra. We have the evidence of Lil Hardin, Armstrong's second wife and one of the major influences on his career, that in his mid-twenties in Chicago, the young Louis did a considerable amount of practising at home. In her own recorded reminiscences ('Lil Armstrong's Own Story', Riverside RLP 12–120), she tells how, when Louis was working with Erskine Tate's Orchestra at the Vendome Theatre and doing a feature number on stage, he ended his solo on a high F, a freakish note to extort from a trumpet in those days. Louis was an instinctual rather than an academic trumpet player and the likelihood is that one night when he was feeling good he simply climbed up to this high note out of sheer recklessness. The word got around that this astonishing virtuoso performance was to be heard, and Louis at home complained to Lil that people were actually coming to the theatre over and over again just to hear him miss that note. He never did miss it, but it worried him. Lil's advice was that of a practical musician. 'All right,' she said, 'c'mon and make some G's at home. If you can make G's in the house, you're not going to worry about hitting F in the theatre!' 'So'—and here the rueful tones of the wife break in on

155

the musician's story—'he was hitting G's at home all day!' It's one of the rare bits of evidence ever found of Louis in his young days actually 'woodshedding' to achieve a specific result on the trumpet.

It's obvious that, from the first lessons in the New Orleans Waifs' Home onwards, he must have worked hard to build the technique and the embouchure to produce the effortless playing which we first hear on record in 1923. But it's equally clear that producing music from the cornet came easy to him, and after the first arduous practice under the tutelage of Mr. Peter Davis at the Waifs' Home, he embarked on no lifelong routine of systematic practice. A trumpeter in a symphony orchestra—or a modern dance band, for that matter—will warm up before a concert with chromatic runs, sustained notes and arpeggios all scientifically designed to loosen up the muscles and make the lip flexible. Louis always had his own way, as anyone who ever lingered enraptured outside his dressing-room door before a concert will know. Indeed, I always looked forward to eavesdropping on this warming-up routine, which was a concert in itself, a free-form potpourri of soaring arpeggios, random quotations from familiar tunes and crackling high notes.

For a musician in the emerging jungle of jazz music in the 'twenties, however supreme his talent, survival meant being prepared at all times to do battle with predatory rivals. There are many tales of the formidable young Louis demolishing the opposition of men like Buddy Petit, Jabbo Smith and 'Hot Lips' Page. My own favourite was again provided by Lil Armstrong. She tells of a night in a Chicago club—in the mid-'twenties, I would guess—when Freddie Keppard, an established hero from New Orleans, tried to give Louis a lesson. After listening to Louis for a while, he said 'Boy, let me have that trumpet.' Then according to Lil, he 'blew and he blew and at the end the people gave him a nice hand. Then he handed the trumpet back to Louis and I said "Get 'im! Get 'im!" Oooh! Never in my life did I hear such trumpet playing. If you want to hear Louis play, hear him when he's angry! Boy, he blew and people started standing up on tables and chairs, screamin'. And Freddie, he just *eased* out!'

The story itself is not unusual in jazz mythology. It is its protracted sequel which sets Louis apart. For his metier was not in the future to be the clubs and joints where such spontaneous battles took place. It was at this very same time that he was practising the high G's at home for his featured number with Erskine Tate at the Vendome Theatre. In telling of this, Lil makes a significant correction in her story. 'I don't remember what number it was he played—anyway, he made a high F on the end.' Then she corrects herself. 'He was *supposed* to make a high F on the end.' It's highly unlikely that any arranger would have written in a high F on the trumpet, and the feat was not common enough in 1926 for band-leader Erskine Tate to have been in a position to insist on it. By whom, then, was Louis 'supposed' to hit the note? By Louis himself, that's my guess. My evidence is in Louis' whole approach to public performance, which he always made perfectly clear by example if not in words.

I've always been intrigued by a purple passage in Mezz Mezzrow's book *Really the Blues* (Secker and Warburg, 1946) which, appalling prose though it is, shows a rare insight into jazz in general and his friend Louis Armstrong in particular. It describes an Armstrong performance in the early 'thirties. Louis was suffering from a chronically sore lip at that time, 'and to make it, he kept at the great sore with a needle . . . his lip looked like he had a big overgrown strawberry setting on it.' There follows a description in almost apocryphal terms of Armstrong's performance of his speciality number, with the staff and chorus girls all crammed into the wings to listen. 'He started to blow his chorus, tearing his heart out, and the tones

157

Freddy Keppard
eases out....

that came vibrating out of those poor agonised lips of his sounded like a weary soul plodding down the lonesome road, the weight of the world's woe on his bent shoulders, crying for relief to all his people.' Mezzrow continues a round by round report in this vein. 'We heard the torture vibrating behind each searing note. The whole theatre was petrified . . . then it happened. Louis began that torturous climb up to high F, the notes all agonised and strangled, each one dripping blood.' (High F's seem to have played a symbolic role in his early career.) 'And then, with the last breath of life left in him, like a man in death convulsions, heaving with his heart and soul and lacerated guts for the last time, Louis clutched and crawled and made that high F on his hands and knees, just barely made it, at the last, nerve-slashing seconds.'

Cynics schooled in the old cliché that a jazz musician plays 'the way he feels' might ask what it was all in aid of. And there is in support of his view the example of generations of jazz musicians—myself among them, I freely confess—who, faced with a nerve-slashing and torturous climb to high F, would have spontaneously 'improvised' an ending on a less exacting low note. Indeed, one might cite, as the furthest extreme from Louis Armstrong's approach, the example of trumpeter Miles Davis who has on many occasions felt so little like playing at all that he has packed up and gone home. But it has to be stressed again and again that Louis Armstrong was not a jazz musician in this legendary sense.

A large part of the disillusionment and overt disappointment expressed by some jazz enthusiasts at hearing Louis Armstrong in the post-war years has arisen from this preconception about a jazz performance. They have grumbled about the unchanging format of his concert repertoire, against which some criticism could fairly be levelled on Louis' own terms. They have also been put off by the absence of fresh improvisation in his solos, by the fact that the same notes and phrases emerged in the same majestically predestined order night after night. But it has been clear ever since those high G's rang out in the living-room of the Armstrong home in Chicago that the hit or miss, play-the-way-I-feel conception of jazz was not his. Nor is there any evidence that it was a part of the New Orleans style of music-making. Jelly Roll Morton thought little of 'improvisers' and kept a strict eye on the variation that musicians applied to his music. King Oliver devised a solo chorus on the Dippermouth Blues which he repeated night after night for his ecstatic audiences—and which other trumpet players have subsequently repeated year after year to the present. Alphonse Picou, having created a clarinet variation on the march 'High Society' by adapting a piccolo part, saw no reason to keep improvising something different. And the two-part cornet breaks with which Joe Oliver and Louis Armstrong surprised the patrons of the Lincoln Gardens in Chicago, though studiously designed to look like spontaneous inventions, were the outcome of a carefully worked-out code—a harmless and entertaining confidence trick, if you like.

It seems, then, that the occasions when Louis cut loose in carefree improvisation were the exception to *his* rule. The wild abandon of some of the Hot Five recordings in the 'twenties can be explained by Louis' own recollection that the musicians didn't take recording seriously. Visits to the studios were a giggling romp in which mistakes often had the epoch-making giants of jazz rolling on the floor and kicking their legs in the air with suppressed mirth. It must have dawned on them, before the decade was out, that the phonograph was not a frivolous sideshow patronised only by crackpots. But at the time, making records, like after-hour 'cutting contests', was an opportunity for letting off creative steam. Years later, Louis said to me, 'I gave up playing for musicians—you can really mess your lip up doin' that!' He didn't say just when this decision was made—it may have been during the period which Mezzrow described, when the Louis lip was like a strawberry. That would have been around 1935, coincidentally the point at which Louis put his career—finances, decision-making and all—in the hands of Joe Glaser.

To many jazz fans who cherish conventional notions of jazz—'I play the way I feel', art for art's sake, let's all get together in a back room—the Louis Armstrong odyssey presents itself as a steady decline into commercialism. Some musicians, too—notably Sidney Bechet, Louis' friend and colleague of the early years—have commented sadly on the course which Louis took. All admit, somewhat grudgingly, that the trumpet-playing, in popular-song recordings, hill-billy hits, Hollywood soundtracks and what-not, retained a remarkable integrity and staying power. They talk as if this were almost an accident, and they may possibly be right. I see it as the end to which Louis Armstrong lived his life—survival. Not the survival of Louis the big star, certainly not of Louis the rich man, but of Louis, the man with a trumpet in his hand. Matching a life-time of playing music through the trumpet with never a tasteless note, never a maladjusted phrase, against the performance of those who died, lapsed into obscurity, burned themselves out or earned their packet and retired, Louis Armstrong's career was a remarkable and formidable exercise of will. In the last years it overcame recurrent illness and the cruel demands of 'show business' in which it was ensnared.

In the light of all this, Louis Armstrong's final appearance in Britain, witnessed in all its detail by his friends here, assumed the elements of Greek tragedy.

When Louis had appeared at the Batley Variety Club in 1968, the fight for survival was still on, though it had become a grim struggle. Reports had filtered down to London after his opening nights that his trumpet playing had become purely vestigial, not more than a few short solo spots in which the tone and timing were all that remained of former glory. Some days later, I was astonished to arrive at the club a few minutes late after tearing up from an engagement in Leeds to hear the familiar solo in 'Indiana', rippling high notes and all, blasting out across the huge auditorium.

Two years and one desperate and weakening illness later, Louis Armstrong came to London for the David Frost concert. To me, he seemed for the first time an old man. The always jaunty, stiff-limbed walk had a frail jerkiness about it and in repose his face wore a crumpled, defeated look. In conversation with friends and in front of an audience, Louis' face always gave an impression of youth, even boyishness. A television interview filmed during his convalescence in 1969 had shown him sitting at his desk looking reassuringly plump in the face and animated. Yet Geoffrey Haydon who conducted the BBC interview said on his return that he had been shocked at the laborious way in which Louis had walked across the room to take a book from the bookshelf, shuffling across the floor without lifting his heels from the ground. When he arrived in London, this frailty was marked—it seemed as if the head of a fifty-year-old was perched on the body of a man of ninety.

Consequently, I was staggered to see him arrive the next morning at the theatre at 11:30, trumpet case not far behind in the hands of a member of his retinue, all ready to rehearse with the orchestra. Now the trumpet notes really were laboured and the effort needed to produce them obviously painful. It is hard to imagine any other artist of international repute in his old age being subjected—or perhaps in Armstrong's case we should still say subjecting himself—to the routine of that day. He had brought Tyree Glenn, the trombonist in his American All Stars, to act as musical director. But it was still Louis who played through all the routines with the orchestra, putting such unconserved energy into his singing that the camera crews, theatre staff and spectators gathered round the stage applauded spontaneously.

162

At 1:30, when rehearsal break arrived, he was hurried to his car and driven to Trafalgar Square so that a film team making a documentary on his progress in collaboration with the Glaser Office—'my own film', Louis called it, to distinguish it from previous documentaries—could shoot him feeding the pigeons. In the Square, there was a repeat of the phenomenon which, at Batley two years earlier, was graphically described by Duggie Tobutt. We were all sitting backstage one day waiting to leave the club when Louis had finished holding court in his dressing room. Duggie shook his head in bewilderment. 'I don't know,' he said, 'here's a guy who goes out and does a show. When he comes off that stage he's just like me at the end of the day—a mean, miserable old bastard who can't wait to get out of the place. But everyone who comes backstage has someone—a sister with three legs, a brother with no arms—and they bring 'em in to see him and he says "Yeah!" and they feel great. What is it with this guy?' In Trafalgar Square, old ladies, bowler-hatted city men and bobbies on the beat, possibly none of whom had ever consciously listened to two bars of jazz, gathered around to shake Louis' hand and tell him about their sons and daughters and sisters and aunts. He was jostled here and there, patted on the back, tugged by the sleeve. At no time was the broad, patient smile switched off or the ear turned away.

It reminded me of an occasion in his dressing-room at the Empress Hall in 1956 when he was buttonholed in a corner by a notorious bore who showed no signs of ever releasing him. His wife Lucille was heard to murmur, 'That guy's boring Louis to death!' and some friends offered to go in and rescue him. 'Oh, don't do that,' she begged earnestly, 'If Louis thinks you don't like the guy, he'll feel sorry for him and talk to him all night!'

Eventually, his managers managed to prize Louis Armstrong away from the crowd in Trafalgar Square and take him back to the Astoria Theatre for further rehearsal. It was after 7 pm when he got away after several run-throughs of the complete show. And by 8:45, he was back ready to go on. No admirer of the genius of Louis Armstrong ever came away from a show without having received some refreshment of the spirit and lightening of the heart. And when Louis talked with David Frost and sang, the old boyishness returned despite signs of strain even in the voice.

But overall, it was a saddening occasion. The gaudy and elaborate stage-setting involved raised glass platforms lit from beneath, across which he had to walk to reach the microphone. Stepping down to floor level, his legs momentarily gave way and he staggered, almost falling over. His show-business reflexes came to the rescue and he covered up with a crack to the effect of 'You want to watch that step!' But he was clearly shaken. And worse was to come. When he started to play the trumpet, it must have been apparent to him before anyone else that the renowned 'chops' had no strength left in them. And the man who caused Freddie Keppard to ease out of that club in Chicago some forty-five years before, and whose majesty on the instrument had never been challenged by any other trumpet-player, surrendered to a ruthless and irresistible opponent and played the trumpet with his back to the audience.